Clear

The Economics and Politics

Answers

of For-Profit Medicine

KEVIN TAFT
&
GILLIAN STEWARD

DUVAL HOUSE PUBLISHING
THE UNIVERSITY OF ALBERTA PRESS
AND
PARKLAND INSTITUTE

PARKLAND
INSTITUTE

DUVAL HOUSE
PUBLISHING

First co-published by:

Duval House Publishing
18120 - 102 Avenue
Edmonton, Alberta, Canada T5S 1S7

The University of Alberta Press
Ring House 2, University of Alberta
Edmonton, Alberta, Canada   T6G 2E1

Parkland Institute
Faculty of Arts, University of Alberta
11044–90 Avenue
Edmonton, Alberta, Canada   T6G 2E1

Order information

Trade Orders:
Raincoast
Phone: 1-800-663-5714
Fax: 1-800-565-3770

Special Orders:
Parkland Institute
Phone: (780) 492-8558
Fax: (780) 492-8738

Copyright © Kevin Taft and Gillian Steward 2000

Layout and production by
Pièce de Résistance Ltée

Printed in Canada   5 4 3 2 1

Canadian Cataloguing in Publication Data

Taft, Kevin, 1955–
  Clear answers

  Copublished by: Parkland Institute, and University of Alberta Press.
  Includes bibliographical references.
  ISBN 1-55220-083-3

  1. Medical care—Alberta—Finance. 2. Medical care—Canada—Finance. 3.
Medical economics—Alberta—Finance. 4. Medical economics—Canada—
Finance. 5. Health care reform—Alberta. 6. Health care reform—Canada. I.
Steward, Gillian, 1946– II. Parkland Institute. III. Title.
RA410.55.C35T33 2000   338.4'33621'097123   C00-910257-4

Duval House Publishing and the University of Alberta Press gratefully
acknowledge the support received for their publishing programs from the
 Department of Canadian Heritage. The Press also gratefully
acknowledges the support received for its program from the
Canada Council for the Arts.

CONTENTS

Acknowledgements vi

Introduction 1

1 The Case for Private,
For-Profit Health Care 5

2 The Evidence 12

3 Your Study Or Mine? 23

4 Creating Crisis 34

5 The Business of Health Care in Calgary 41

6 Jim Dinning Prepares the Way
for Privatization 49

7 A Glimpse Into For-Profit Medicine 54

8 HRG: The Edge of the Wedge 67

9 The Outer Limits 77

10 The Entrepreneurial Doctors 86

11 Questions and Answers 93

12 The Cure is the Disease 106

Appendix A: The Numbers
Behind the Graphs 109

Appendix B: Trends in Provincial Government
Health Spending 114

Appendix C: Health Spending
as a Portion of GDP 116

Bibliography 117

About the Authors 122

ACKNOWLEDGEMENTS

THIS BOOK HAS COME together quickly and smoothly, and credit for that must be generously shared. The Parkland Institute's role in launching the initial research and maintaining high academic standards has been vital. The team of publishers, editors, reviewers, and designers has performed to perfection. Gillian has cherished the keen sense of justice and unwavering support of her husband, Terry Steward. None of this would have happened without the remarkable people who have volunteered time and expertise to work with heart and soul to defend Canada's medicare system, especially here in Alberta. They have provided unwavering moral support and a flow of articles, tips, ideas, and passion that have sustained and inspired the writing. Thank you. Your dedication is humbling; all Canadians should be grateful.

Kevin Taft and *Gillian Steward*

TO JEANETTE

who has been my most valued and trusted supporter, every step of the way. Thanks, my love,

Kevin

TO MY FATHER

William J. Cranley (1914–1980), one of those doctors who went on strike in Saskatchewan in 1962 but later became a staunch defender of Canadian medicare.

Gillian

INTRODUCTION

A reasonable question, a clear answer

In early December, 1999, both *Time* magazine and the *Globe and Mail* published personal editorials by Premier Klein of Alberta. They sketch out his proposal "...that private clinics be allowed to contract with regional health authorities for procedures that require overnight stays." Mr. Klein uses the term "clinics," but most people believe places in which patients have major surgery and stay for a period of days to recover with medical and nursing care are hospitals. Acknowledging that his proposal is controversial, he writes, "At least, let's have the discussion" (*Time*, 6 Dec. 1999, p52).

A discussion about opening Canada's public system of health care, or "medicare," to private for-profit hospitals is a discussion not just for Albertans, but for all Canadians. In every province and territory people are debating the future of medicare, and just as the possibility of turning to for-profit hospitals is now being considered by the Alberta government, it will be considered elsewhere.

Questions about the value and merits of for-profit health care are not new. Theories have been developed, tested, and revised in countless studies. For several decades and across many parts of the world, the answer has been impressively consistent: market forces in health care drive costs up and overall efficiencies down.

Governments need the guts occasionally to round-up every sacred cow, to challenge conventional wisdom and assumed truth. Having asked the tough questions, they need to search for the best answers, and to accept those answers. The Government of Alberta under Ralph Klein has asked a pointed but reasonable question: can health care be better provided partly as a private, for-profit product rather than as a not-for-profit public service?

It now has the responsibility to seriously examine the evidence, and to accept what it reveals: that health care is not an ordinary commodity that fits well into market economics. Health care does not lend itself to for-profit management and delivery. It is an example of what economists call "market failure": the market fails to produce and distribute health care effectively and efficiently.

Early lessons in health economics

My first serious look into the role of market forces in health care came in the early 1980s. There was then a sharp debate in some provinces about user fees for health-care services. The Alberta government favoured user fees as an option for controlling costs, on the principle that requiring patients to pay a small fee would encourage them to think twice before visiting a doctor. The federal government and a range of other groups were opposed to them.

I was hired by a branch of the Alberta government to study the issue. With my freshly minted Masters degree and an earnest desire to do a "professional" job, I set off to read up on all sides of the issue. The logic of user fees seemed clear enough, and I expected to find studies showing that they worked as planned.

I was in for a surprise. Every study I found showed much the opposite: user fees do not reduce total costs, nor do they lower overall demand on the health-care system. They discourage the elderly and the poor, people who often need help the most, from visiting doctors. Any capacity freed up by reduction in demand is quickly filled with services initiated by physicians, such as minor surgeries, and by people for whom user fees are no barrier: the middle and upper classes.

I quickly learned two important lessons. First: health care does not respond in the usual way to the laws of supply, demand, and price. Second: private, for-profit, market-driven medicine is both costly and unfair.

While many public issues present genuine puzzles and dilemmas (think of, say, locating garbage dumps, responding to youth crime, or balancing environmental issues) there was a striking clarity and consistency in studies of health economics: study after study—decade after decade and in country after country—has found that health care is a market failure. I described these findings in my report and advised that user fees weren't a useful way to control health-care costs. The report was well-received, I was congratulated on a job well done, and I was paid. Then I learned a third lesson: governments don't necessarily take good advice. Like the rest of us, when their minds are made up they don't like to be confused with the facts. My report was shelved. The provincial government didn't end extra billing by doctors until a political battle with the federal government in 1986, and then it allowed hospital user fees to evolve into the "facility fees" now charged by private day-surgery clinics.

●●●

Since that first study in the early 1980s, I have returned from time to time to monitor the debates on private, for-profit versus public non-profit health systems. The number of studies have multiplied, and their quality has grown steadily better. I have continued to search material on both sides of the issue. The only major change over the years is that the evidence against relying on market forces in health care is more widespread than ever. In this book I provide a sample and a summary of the evidence, and I try to do it in a way that is clear, readable, and accurate.

As I write this, despite its invitation to "have the discussion," the Klein government gives every indication that its mind is made up. It seems about to ignore tremendous evidence. It has issued a declaration that the role of for-profit medicine will be substantially increased in Alberta, and it has launched an extraordinary public relations campaign to support its position. It doesn't want a discussion, it wants a victory. The Premier, who is personally leading the campaign, has acknowledged that he faces a tough fight on the issue.

Governments don't risk tough political fights without reasons, especially when the best evidence and arguments are massed against them. This book not only presents the arguments, it also looks for explanations of Mr. Klein's actions. Why, in his own words, has he "decided to touch the electrified third rail of Canadian politics"? If, as the research consistently shows, for-profit medicine cannot be described as being in the public interest, then in whose interest is it? To help shed light on this, Gillian Steward describes some of the behind-the-scenes politics and relationships in Alberta's health-care industry. With clear answers and expert evidence ranged so overwhelmingly against for-profit health care, and with some influential Albertans invested so heavily in for-profit health-care projects, we face a moment in our history when Alberta's leaders, the Klein government, will need to make a clear choice between private profit and public interest. Other governments in Canada will soon face the same decision.

Kevin Taft, February 2000

1

THE CASE

FOR PRIVATE,

FOR-PROFIT

HEALTH CARE

EARLY IN HIS CAMPAIGN to promote the privatization of overnight surgical services Ralph Klein worked on getting his message into nation-wide media. One of these media was CBC-Television's "The National Magazine." When viewers tuned into the program on the evening of 6 December 1999, their screens flashed with the headline "The Klein Cure," then cut to a shot of the host, Brian Stewart:

> BRIAN STEWART: *"Tonight: an Alberta plan puts Canadian health care at a crossroads: let private hospitals do major surgeries."*
>
> UNIDENTIFIED SPEAKER: *"Health care is not a commodity. It's part of a caring society."*
>
> SECOND UNIDENTIFIED SPEAKER: *"It is a commodity, like it or not."*

In a few phrases, these two unidentified speakers touched the essential dilemma at the heart of so much debate over health care. Is health care a product like any other, to be bought and sold like a bushel of wheat or a hamburger? Or is it something different, something that requires special considerations? If health care is an ordinary commodity, then steps to increase free markets and competition in the health-care system could bring market benefits, such as lower costs. On the other hand, if health care is not an ordinary commodity, for-profit competition could lead to serious troubles.

In "The National Magazine" broadcast, the speaker describing health care as a commodity turns out to be Dr. Steve Miller, an orthopedic surgeon and the Chief Medical Officer of a Calgary-based company called Health Resources Group, or HRG. HRG operates clinics that do minor day surgeries. They want to expand into major surgeries that require overnight stays, such as hip replacements, creating what most people would describe as for-profit hospitals. For those who regard health care as a commodity, health-care delivery should be transferred increasingly to the private sector, where for-profit companies will compete with one another to deliver services. A competitive market, says this argument, will create an efficient, innovative, and responsive system of health care that will provide the greatest benefits to the most patients at the lowest costs, while simultaneously profiting shareholders. Those who regard health care as a commodity will find much to support in the initiatives of the Klein government.

The marketplace and medicare

The arguments in favour of increasing for-profit market forces in Canada's health-care system are clearly presented in David Gratzer's 1999 book, *Code Blue*. For Gratzer, the physician-patient relationship is fundamentally an economic one, like the seller-buyer relationship for any other commodity. In his view, Canadians have made a serious mistake by allowing their medicare system to remove the money basis of the doctor-patient relationship: "*[T]he fundamental flaw of the medicare system is that patients bear no direct costs for the medical services they receive*...the problem lies in the fact that the doctor-patient relationship has been corrupted by the "free" nature of the system" (emphasis in original; pp 118, 137).

Gratzer and other advocates of private, for-profit health care argue that competitive markets have produced an abundance of inexpensive, high-quality, and widely-available food, shelter, and clothing, and that competitive markets would do the same for Canada's health-care system, if only the constraints of medicare were lifted. Gratzer says a free market could offer many advantages over medicare:

With health care, government has corrupted the market. Consider that, in a normal market, problems are solved by consumers and producers pursuing their own self interests. Consumers tend to avoid waste and inefficiency because they usually result in higher prices. Instead, consumers seek good products at attractive prices offered by efficient suppliers. Producers search for less costly ways of delivering wanted goods—they reduce inefficiencies and develop innovative approaches. Pursuit of self-interest by consumers rewards efficient producers, and pursuit of self-interest by producers rewards cost-conscious consumers.

But these normal market processes—based on productive self-interest, if you will—have been replaced for health care by bureaucratic institutions, and normal market incentives have been replaced by bureaucratic rule making. (pp 172–173).

Food is an example of a successful free-market product often cited in introductory economics textbooks, and used by Gratzer as an analogy for health care. Food, like health care, is a basic need, and much of the food industry is run through private, for-profit markets, with impressive results.

> *We can purchase an incredible variety of quality food, from the exotic cuisine of foreign lands to the wholesome goodness of locally grown flour... [F]ood is always readily available, even in the wee hours of the morning... [M]ost restaurants and grocery stores are cost effective; if not, they go bankrupt... [F]ood is produced to be sold, so producers have a strong incentive to meet the needs and desires of consumers... [A]ll Canadians have access to basic foods. True, not everyone can afford caviar and lox, but no one starves.* (p171).

Medical savings accounts

Gratzer is by no means alone in arguing that health care should be opened to market forces, and there are many ideas about how it should be done. Gratzer himself, drawing on the work and experience of others, proposes a scheme of "Medical Savings Accounts." Medical savings accounts (MSAs) have two basic components. First, people are required to have insurance covering their health care costs above a certain amount each year, typically $2,000. This insurance looks after all major expenses a person may face. Second, that amount ($2,000, for example) is paid every year into each person's MSA, either by an employer or through a mandatory payroll deduction. People can use the money in their MSAs for any health-related expense they choose: doctors appointments, physiotherapy, medications, and so on. If they don't spend all the money in their MSAs by the end of the year they can keep it for themselves or allow it to accumulate in their MSAs.

The theory behind an MSA system is that the insurance protects a person from the catastrophic expenses of major illness, while the savings account gives enough consumer choice to generate market forces in the health-care system. People will be motivated to shop around for the best prices on health care and to avoid unnecessary treatments because they can keep the surplus in their account at the end of each year. MSAs have been tried on a small scale in some parts of the United States, and on a nation-wide scale in Singapore.

Internal markets

A different approach to increasing the role of market forces in health care is to create "internal markets." These have been attempted in Europe, most notably in Britain's National Health Service (NHS). With internal markets, organizations within a public, not-for-profit system compete with each other to provide services. For instance, a public health-care agency may ask various public hospitals to bid against each other to provide services in a particular region, and the hospitals may then compete on the basis of costs and services to gain the contract. Similarly, a public health-insurance plan may request clinics to compete with one another by submitting plans to care for patients in particular regions. The successful clinics may in turn seek competing bids from public hospitals to provide hospital services to the clinics' patients.

If internal markets were implemented in Alberta, for example, you might see the Department of Health requesting hospitals in Calgary or Edmonton to submit bids to provide pediatric services. The hospitals offering the best services at the lowest prices would win the contract. As well, clinics might be asked by the Alberta Health Insurance Plan to submit plans to care for patients in their region: perhaps southwest Calgary, or Grande Prairie, for instance. In return for providing care to these patients, the clinic would be paid a certain amount. Those clinics could then ask hospitals to bid against each other to provide selected services (such as MRIs or chemotherapy) to the clinics' patients. Each clinic would negotiate the best contract it could with hospitals, presumably acting on its patients' best interests.

Contracting out

With a system of internal markets, the competition remains within the public sector. With contracting out, contracts occur between the public system and private, for-profit service providers. Contracting out of non-clinical functions such as laundry and dietary services has been common for decades. In these non-clinical areas, *if* there are several qualified bidders in true competition for a contract with a hospital, the hospital may benefit from market forces.

But a new area of contracting out has arisen recently in Alberta, involving direct clinical services such as day surgery. This raises new complications, because it creates a situation where the incomes of the clinical service providers are directly linked to the clinical choices they make. While a laundry contractor has little influence over the amount of laundry used in a hospital, contractors providing clinical services may well be able to influence the demand for the procedures they provide, through what they prescribe or recommend for their patients. Differing views on contracting out clinical services lie at the core of much of the debate around the

Klein government's initiatives on private clinics and hospitals.

Many private options, one conclusion

There have been many other attempts to argue for a role for market forces in health care. For example, in 1979, the Fraser Institute published a book by economist Ake Blomquist calling for an end to publicly subsidized health insurance and health services, and for a new system of compulsory private insurance and market-based hospital services for Canada (Blomquist 1979).

In the United States, where the effects of market forces on health care are most strongly felt, huge hospital corporations vie for patients, pharmaceutical companies own many medical clinics, for-profit insurance companies have enormous influence on the demand for and supply of health care, and for-profit Health Maintenance Organizations (HMOs) manage huge, diverse, private systems.

There is no shortage of experience in mixing health care and market forces. Does it work? Is health care an economic commodity like hamburgers, obeying the rules of the marketplace? Is private health care cheaper and more efficient than public health care? Which system serves more people better at lower cost? These are questions that can be—and have been—studied and answered, over, and over, and over. There is enough evidence about the role of market forces in health care to fill shelves of books. The results are clear and overwhelming, and in Alberta the Klein government has so far chosen to ignore it all.

2

THE EVIDENCE

ON 1 DECEMBER 1999, shortly after 1:50 pm, Alberta opposition leader Nancy MacBeth stood during question period in the Legislature to ask Premier Ralph Klein for his response to a study published in the *New England Journal of Medicine* on 5 August 1999. The study found that when hospitals in the US converted from non-profit to for-profit status, their costs rose markedly. Premier Klein responded:

> *Mr. Speaker, without wanting to sound repetitive, it is that kind of information, that kind of fear-mongering that leads to public confusion relative to this issue.*

It was the beginning of a heated and prolonged exchange in which neither Premier Klein nor his Minister of Health and Wellness, Halvar Jonson, spoke to the findings of the study (*Alberta Hansard*).

What did the *New England Journal of Medicine* say? Its 5 August 1999 issue carried two articles relevant to the debate in Alberta. One was a special editorial providing an overview of the evidence concerning the costs of investor-owned for-profit hospitals. "For decades," its first paragraph states, "studies have shown that for-profit hospitals are 3 to 11 percent more expensive than not-for-profit hospitals; no peer-reviewed study has found that for-profit hospitals are less expensive."

It notes that in regions of the US where investor-owned hospitals dominate, US Medicare (the government program that provides health services to people over age 65) pays more not only for hospital care but also for home care and care in other facilities. The article also cited examples of huge marketing budgets, big executive bonuses, and questionable billing practices at for-profit hospitals, and noted several studies that found for-profit hospitals provide lower quality of care (Woolhandler and Himmelstein, 1999).

The second relevant article in the August 5 issue of the *New England Journal of Medicine* compares Medicare spending in for-profit hospitals and not-for-profit hospitals in the US. The study's findings are clear: in every category of service examined—hospital services, physicians' services, home health care, and services at other facilities—Medicare spending was 13 percent to 16 percent higher when it was connected to for-profit hospitals than when it was connected to not-for profit hospitals In addition, spending was increasing faster in areas served by for-profit hospitals than in areas served by not-for-profit hospitals; in other words, the cost gap between for-profit and not-for profit care was growing. "Our findings are consistent," the study concludes, "with the possibility that for-profit hospital ownership itself contributes to higher per capita costs for the Medicare population served by these hospitals" (p425). The study covers all fifty states in the US, and it takes into account a wide range of variables, such as age and race differences, and urbanization rates (Silverman, Skinner, and Fisher).

Given his invitation to "have the discussion," it is surprising that Alberta's Premier was evasive when asked about these articles in the Legislature. But these two articles are just the tip of the iceberg: the evidence contradicting the Premier's position is overwhelming. When put to the hard test of reality, the case for supporting private, for-profit medicine does not come off well:

1999:

A study comparing waiting lists and costs for cataract surgery in Alberta found that costs were highest and waiting lists longest in regions dominated by private clinics. In Calgary, which had the most eye surgeons in the province, 100 percent of cataract surgery was done in private clinics. Waiting lists averaged 16 to 24 weeks and the most common extra charge to patients was $400 per eye for upgraded lenses. In Edmonton, where there were fewer eye surgeons, 80 percent of cataract surgery was done in public hospitals. Waiting lists averaged five to seven weeks and the most common charge for an upgraded lens was $250 per eye. In Lethbridge, where 100 percent of cataract surgery was done in public facilities, the average wait was four to seven weeks and there was no extra charge for the upgraded lens, which was purchased by the regional health authority for well under $100. The study was carried out by the Alberta Branch of the Consumers' Association of Canada, a non-profit consumer advocacy group (Consumers' Association of Canada [Alberta Branch] May 1999; March 1999).

1999:

The *Journal of the American Medical Association* reports a study which raises serious concerns about the quality of care in investor-owned for-profit Health Maintenance Organizations (HMOs) in the US, when compared to not-for-profit HMOs. The implications of the study are serious, say its authors: "[I]f all 23.7 million American women between the ages 50 and 69 were enrolled in investor-owned, rather than not-for-profit plans, an estimated 5925 additional breast cancer deaths would be expected" (p162). They go on to say, "[T]he decade old experiment with market medicine is a failure. The drive for profit is compromising the quality of care, the number of uninsured persons is increasing, those with insurance are increasingly dissatisfied, bureaucracy is proliferating, and costs are again rapidly escalating" (Himmelstein et al., p163).

Investor-owned HMOs scored lower on all 14 quality-of-care indicators used in the study: "[I]nvestor-ownership was consistently associated with lower quality after controlling for model type, geographic region, and the method each HMO used to collect data" (p159). While the study found that costs per member were virtually identical in the two types of HMOs, "[S]pending on administration and profit was about 48% higher in investor-owned plans (19.4% vs. 13.1% for not-for-profit plans)" (p162). The study was based on 1997 Health Plan Employer Data from 329 HMOs, accounting for over one-half of HMO registrations in the US.

1999:

A large study comparing for-profit and not-for-profit kidney dialysis centers in the United States found that the death rate of patients in for-profit centers was 20 percent higher than in not-for-profit centers. The study tracked more than 3,500 dialysis patients, for from three to six years. About two-thirds of the estimated 200,000 dialysis patients in the US go to for-profit dialysis centres, which receive significant funding from a special US Medicare program. The findings were consistent with several smaller studies suggesting that for-profit dialysis centres offer lower quality of care. An editorial in the *New England Journal of Medicine*, in which the study was published, stated, "[T]he study provides important data about the influence of commercial ownership of dialysis facilities on the quality of care" (Garg, et al.).

1997:

"Contrary to the rhetoric of the market, market forces are apparently "upsizing" administration" in private, for-profit hospitals, concluded a huge study published in the *New England Journal of Medicine* (p774). The study, which conducted a detailed analysis of over 5,000 US hospitals, found that for-profit hospitals spend 34 percent of their total budgets on administration, compared to 22.9 percent in US public hospitals. For-profit hospitals also have higher costs per inpatient day and per discharge (Woolhandler and Himmelstein, 1997).

Part of the study compared hospital spending in 1990 and 1994, and found that the biggest increases in administration costs were in for-profit hospitals, which had the highest rates to begin with. The study also notes that even before the increases of the 1990s, hospital administration costs in the US were nearly twice as high as in Canada. The researchers also found that hospitals which converted from non-profit to for-profit status during the course of the study had much higher increases in administration than those that converted from for-profit to not-for-profit.

Why did for-profit hospitals do the poorest job of containing administration costs? "It may be incorrect to equate market success with efficiency," said the study. "Business strategies unrelated or even detrimental to efficiency can bolster profitability and market share" (p774). These strategies include providing financial incentives to physicians to use their services, and "upcoding" diagnoses.

> *Many [people] assume that the growth of for-profit hospitals in the United States is attributable to lower costs and greater efficiency and that competitive pressures are wringing administrative excess from hospitals. Studies based on figures from the 1970s and early 1980s, however, found higher total costs at for-profit hospitals, largely because they charged more for ancillary services and spent more on administration.* (p769)

This study confirms and updates those earlier findings.

The authors of the study suggest they are *under*stating the full costs of for-profit hospitals, since their study omits profits, many marketing costs, and the "entrepreneurial expenses" that US Medicare excludes from reimbursement. The study used detailed statistical analyses of hospital billing data, and corrected for variables such as number of beds per hospital, type of care provided, and type of hospital.

1995:

An evaluation of the implementation of "internal markets" in Britain's National Health Service (NHS) found that "...the introduction of market-based reforms was accompanied by the fastest increase in spending on the NHS since the 1960s." The reforms did assist in loosening some of the highly centralized control of the NHS, and improved the responsiveness of hospitals to doctors and patients (Glennester, p23).

The internal market reforms "...have not substantially reduced the numbers waiting for at least a year for elective procedures, and they have required substantial additional funds to cover the larger transaction costs of a price-based health market." In fact, introducing competitive incentives has actually increased the need for regulation (Saltman, p82).

Market-based reforms to Britain's NHS have consumed substantial resources, "...but evidence about the gains they have produced is sparse." These reforms have raised ethical concerns: "[T]he commercialization of medicine poses major ethical threats: if doctors own facilities, for example, they may create unnecessary demand for patient care and income for their bank accounts" (Maynard, p40; p34).

The ability-to-pay principle "...is dominant in many markets for goods and services but has generally been abandoned in health care markets.... The abandonment of this principle is a product of market failures that have proved impossible to remedy in practice but that are still deemed soluble by market-oriented reformers..." (Maynard, p28).

Even Ake Blomquist, who wrote a book for the Fraser Institute in 1979 advocating a huge shift toward market forces in Canada's health-care system, concedes that "...anyone who argues in favour of reforms based on internal markets at the present time does so largely on faith. The amount of hard evidence on whether, in reality, internal market reforms would lead to substantial efficiency gains (net of transaction costs) is still very limited" (Blomquist [1995], p183).

1995:

A decade after implementing medical savings accounts

in order to increase market forces in its health-care system, the government of Singapore has concluded , "The health care system is an example of market failure." Singapore, which has a high level of economic development, had until 1985 a tax-funded health-care system derived from the original British model. That year, in an effort to control costs and improve efficiency, the government introduced MSAs, hoping that market forces would work in health care as they do in other areas (Hsiao, p265).

Instead of slowing the growth in health expenditures, market forces drove spending up more rapidly. By one measure—the number of patient days per staff—efficiency improved, but by other important measures it declined. Private hospitals did not compete by reducing costs, but by offering the latest and most expensive equipment. An evaluation of the MSAs concluded, "Ten years after the reform, Singapore is saddled with widespread duplication of expensive medical equipment and high-technology services," including seven in-vitro fertilization programs for a population of 3.3 million.

The same evaluation found:

Under a free market the fees and incomes of private-sector physicians rose at a phenomenal rate, which caused experienced physicians to migrate from the public to the private sector. The public sector had to raise compensation for its physicians and other health care workers to retain well-qualified professionals in the public sector....(p265)

1993:

A study of data from more than 6,000 hospitals in the

United States concluded that "...more competitive bidding by hospitals for managed-care contracts, an important element of proposed managed-competition health care reforms, does not lower hospital administrative costs" (p400). The study found that, ironically, "In many hospitals, as the number of patients declined, the number of bureaucrats increased to battle with competing hospitals over market share and with insurers over payment" (p401). The research also revealed that, "Hospital administrative costs in the United States are higher than previous estimates and more than twice as high as those in Canada" (p400). (Woolhandler, Himmelstein, and Lewontin).

Published in the *New England Journal of Medicine*, the study concluded by saying, "Our...findings yield no evidence that managed care and competitive bidding, as envisioned under a managed-competition strategy, will prune hospital administration" (p401).

1986:

Researchers who compared not-for-profit hospitals with investor-owned hospital chains found the investor-owned hospitals increased their profits by raising prices rather than improving efficiencies. Writing in the *New England Journal of Medicine*, the researchers said their results "...strongly suggest the existence of a strategy by the investor-owned chain hospitals of setting competitive prices for the more visible "room and board" services while setting higher prices for ancillary services, which are less easy to compare from hospital to hospital" (p95). Pharmaceutical and medical supplies were identified in the research as especially prone to aggressive pricing (Watt, et al.).

The higher prices in for-profit hospitals contributed

to a cost per admission that was 22 percent higher than in not-for-profit hospitals. "[I]nvestor-owned hospitals [were] more costly to patients and third-party payers, but not more efficient than their not-for-profit counterparts," said the study (p94). The researchers noted that their findings were consistent with several previous studies showing for-profit hospitals cost 15 to 23 percent more than non-profit hospitals.

The study analyzed 80 matched pairs of investor-owned chain hospitals and not-for-profit hospitals, and adjusted for the cost of taxes to investor-owned hospitals.

1983:

A careful statistical analysis using data on 280 California hospitals found that for-profit hospitals made much heavier use of high-mark-up areas, especially pharmacies and labs, than did voluntary and public hospitals, increasing the profitability of for-profit hospitals. Because of the profitability of those services, some routine services and procedures could be marketed as "loss leaders." Basic room rates, for example, could be lowered. (Pattison and Katz).

The study found that for-profit hospitals had two to six percent higher operating costs per patient day, and substantially higher administrative costs than not-for-profit and public hospitals. The researchers said their data "...do not support the claim that investor-owned chains enjoy overall operating efficiencies or economies of scale in administrative or fiscal services" (pp 351–352).

This study, published in the *New England Journal of Medicine*, found that for-profit hospitals admitted more emergency room visitors for hospital stays, although they were not treating more complex patients. The researchers said this lends credence "...to concerns that the tension between profit maximization and medical appropriateness may lead to different styles of medical practice in these hospitals" (p350).

● ● ●

The evidence cited above is just a small sample of a huge number of studies. Their results are powerfully consistent: health care is not a commodity like others. It does not benefit from market-based reforms. For-profit competition increases costs, drives up administrative inefficiencies, creates barriers to equal access for all people, and can threaten quality of care. Private, for-profit health care has been proven conclusively to be a bad idea for almost everyone. If we really have the discussion in Alberta and Canada, that's how the discussion has to conclude, unless it ignores the facts.

3

YOUR STUDY

OR MINE?

AFTER RALPH KLEIN said opposition leader Nancy MacBeth was fear-mongering in that 1 December 1999 question period, he sat down and she rose with further questions. Several minutes of increasingly strained debate ticked by, and then moments after 2:00 pm, Nancy MacBeth asked:

Why won't the Premier consider overwhelming evidence that his privatization scheme may lead to increased health care costs for the citizens of Alberta?

Ralph Klein answered:

Mr. Speaker, as I said before, at the risk of getting into the game of I'll show you your study; you show me my study, there are studies going back and forth. There is a lot of evidence both ways. We have the policy statement out there for public discussion. We want to make sure before we introduce legislation that it's absolutely right.

After more exchanges Nancy MacBeth asked:

According to the Center for Health Program Studies at Harvard Medical School…administration costs in the private US system are four times what they are in Canada under the public system…. My question is: how much does the Premier plan to see administration costs go up under the scheme that he wants to introduce for privatization here in Alberta? Where's his study?

Ralph Klein answered:

Mr. Speaker, obviously, I'm not getting through to the opposition. They can't understand. But, you know, our Minister of Health and Wellness used to be a school teacher, and perhaps he can stand up and explain the policy, perhaps in grade 5 language. I'll defer to the Honourable Minister. (Alberta Hansard)

Let's look at the Premier's claim that "...there are studies going back and forth. There is a lot of evidence both ways." It is true that many books and articles have been written arguing that market forces and for-profit business should be increased in health care. These include a report sometimes mentioned by the Premier called *Operating in the Dark: The Gathering Crisis in Canada's Public Health Care System*, by the Atlantic Institute for Market Studies; David Gratzer's *Code Blue*; and articles in the *Fraser Forum*, published by The Fraser Institute (see Crowley, Zitner, and Faraday-Smith; Gratzer; McArthur; Zenter, 1999).

But arguing that market forces should be increased is not the same as showing evidence that market-driven health care works. For example, in a feature column titled "Let's End the Nonprofit Charade" published in 1996 in the *New England Journal of Medicine*, physician Malik Hasan writes, "The market can and will resolve all outstanding health care issues" (Hasan). This kind of writing may be easier to read than pages of technical data, but it isn't good research.

Many of the studies showing the inadequacies and costs of for-profit health care use proven methods of scientific analysis, are statistically validated, and come to conclusions that are precise and measurable. They are carefully reviewed by independent committees and published in credible journals. Comparing the material arguing in favour of market medicine with that in favour of public non-profit medicare seems often like comparing circumstantial evidence with direct evidence. Mr. Klein can match the Opposition anecdote for anecdote and sound bite for sound bite, but he can't match the Opposition's valid research.

• • •

Sometimes authors supporting privatized health care seem so committed to their positions that they risk misinterpreting the evidence. David Gratzer's book *Code Blue* provides an interesting example. *Code Blue* gives a long critique of Canada's medicare system, and then argues that Canada should introduce market forces into medicare through medical savings accounts (MSAs). One of the few places where MSAs have been tried on a widespread basis is Singapore. Gratzer describes Singapore's experience in part this way:

> *It's difficult to judge the success of Singapore's health care system… Still, some crude analysis can be done. The wages of doctors in Singapore are on par with those of doctors in the United States and higher than those of doctors in Canada (see Hsiao). Diagnostic medical equipment, such as CT and MRI scanners, is more abundant in Singapore than in Canada….* (p203)

One of the two sources Gratzer uses for his analysis of Singapore is an article published in the respected journal *Health Affairs* in 1995 by William Hsiao, an economist from Harvard. Despite the impression Gratzer creates, Hsiao's article is rather negative about the effects of MSAs and markets on health delivery in Singapore. Here is a small portion of what Hsiao's article actually says:

> *Singapore's decade-long experience shows that its MSAs neither reduced nor controlled health care cost inflation. Instead, cost inflation rates increased....*
>
> *Singapore found that hospitals largely did not compete on price. For example, the average charge of private hospitals for an appendectomy was twice that of the prestigious Singapore General Hospital. Hospitals competed instead by offering the latest technology and expensive equipment.... Ten years after the reform [i.e. the introduction of MSAs], Singapore is saddled with widespread duplication of expensive medical equipment and high-technology services....*
>
> *Under a free market the fees and incomes of private-sector physicians rose at a phenomenal rate, which caused experienced physicians to migrate to the private sector. The public sector had to raise compensation for its physicians and other health care workers to retain well-qualified professionals in the public sector. Today, the top surgeons employed by the public hospitals receive close to $400,000 per year. Top private-sector surgeons earn at least twice that amount. Rapidly rising compensation was another cause of health care cost inflation.* (pp 260, 264, 265)

● ● ●

A report by the Fraser Institute provides another example of how results of research can be arrayed to create impressions that may be misleading. According to its website, the Fraser Institute "...was founded in 1974 to redirect public attention to the role markets can play in providing for the economic and social well-being of Canadians." Not surprisingly, the report it has produced favours more privatization and stronger market forces in Canada's health-care system. The report, titled "How Private Hospital Competition Can Improve Canadian Health Care," was released by the Fraser Institute in January 2000, specifically to support the Klein government's initiative on private hospitals (Zelder, 2000). It creates the impression that a good deal of research shows private for-profit hospitals "perform better" than non-profit and public hospitals. For example, in its interpretation of the research it says, "Undoubtedly the most germane information is the substantial empirical support for the proposition that for-profit hospitals are lower-cost than government hospitals."

This is well worth closer investigation in view of statements to the complete opposite by so many others, including the prestigious American National Academy of Sciences' Institute of Medicine in 1986, the respected journal *Health Affairs* in 1997, and the *New England Journal of Medicine* in 1999. Something does not add up (see Gray, 1986a; Anderson; Woolhandler and Himmelstein, 1999).

This Fraser Institute report uses various studies to support its claims for the superiority of for-profit hospitals. When these claims of The Fraser Institute were compared against some of the original research papers they cite, discrepancies turned up:

First

The first article used by The Fraser Institute to show better performance by for-profit hospitals was written in 1972. The Fraser Institute says its author, Kenneth Clarkson, "...determined that government hospitals performed worse" than for-profits in selected ways, including providing less employee supervision and higher rates of automatic salary increases.

A check of the Clarkson article reveals that it does not say "government hospitals performed worse," but rather that for-profit and not-for-profit hospitals behave differently. The Fraser Institute does not mention that Clarkson found non-profit hospitals more likely to have formal budgets approved by boards; more likely to have written staff regulations; more likely to have regularly scheduled staff meetings; more likely to have restrictions on non-staff members practicing in the hospital; more likely to have administrators who were graduates of college hospital administration courses; and more likely to have administrators who were members of the American College of Hospital Administrators.

In any case, the article is so old and limited as to be irrelevant today. The data showing that for-profit hospitals supervise staff more closely is from a survey done in 1953; the information that not-for-profits give more automatic raises comes from a 1956 survey.

Second

The Fraser Institute is correct when it says a study by Wilson and Jadlow (1982) found private hospitals were more efficient than public ones in using staff and capital to provide nuclear medicine services (eg. radiology). This study had one other major finding: competition among hospitals has a "perverse effect" on efficiency: "[A]s hospital market structure becomes more competitive...the hospitals in the market will become less efficient". The Fraser Institute does not mention this second finding, even in their discussion of the effects of competition on hospital performance.

Third

The Fraser Institute summarizes the findings of Robinson and Luft (1985) in one sentence: "They discovered that for-profits had significantly lower cost per admission and per day than non-profits."

A different impression is created by Robinson and Luft themselves, who summarize their own findings this way: "Using data from hospitals in 1972 we analyzed the impact of market structure on average hospital costs, measured in terms of both cost per patient and cost per patient day. Under the retrospective reimbursement system in place at the time, hospitals in more competitive environments exhibited significantly higher costs of production than did those in less competitive environments."

In their conclusion, Robinson and Luft say, "The findings support the hypothesis that... greater competition is associated with higher rather than lower costs." As with the preceding study, this conclusion is not mentioned in The Fraser Institute's discussion on hospital competition.

Fourth

According to The Fraser Institute, a study by Hoerger (1991) is, "a subtle test of non-profit inefficiency" which "implicitly [confirms] ...that non-profits maintain more slack." In fact, Hoerger's study is *not* a test of "non-profit inefficiency", nor does he conclude that non-profit hospitals are inefficient. His hypothesis is that "...government and private not-for-profit hospitals behave differently than for-profit hospitals," especially in the face of financial restrictions, which his study confirms.

FIFTH

In an example that is particularly relevant for the impact of Klein's proposals on rural Alberta, The Fraser Institute correctly says a study of rural American hospitals by Ferrier and Valdmanis (1996) shows "for-profits were efficient compared to non-profits" according to three of the four measures of efficiency they used. The Fraser Institute does not mention that Ferrier and Valdmanis seriously discuss the possibility that this may be because "...for-profit hospitals may choose to operate only in areas where returns on investment are likely to accrue," while public hospitals serve areas where optimal efficiency may not be possible, but where medical services are nonetheless needed.

SIXTH

The Fraser Institute claims a 1997 article by Altman and Shactman in the *New England Journal of Medicine* indicates "better performance by for-profits." Altman and Shactman's short article argues that high administrative costs in hospitals are not necessarily bad if they lead to better administration. They cite an unpublished study showing that for-profit hospitals in the US, which typically have higher administrative costs than non-profit hospitals, have "reduced their cost per case relative to their not-for-profit and public hospital counterparts."

What The Fraser Institute does not include is that

Altman and Shactman follow this point by raising the issue at the heart of their discussion: "If the rate of cost increase is declining at for-profit hospitals, what is being sacrificed in return? Have for-profit hospitals been able to increase efficiency, or have they achieved savings by reducing the quality of care, the amount of charity care and community benefits, or the provision of services? These are the questions we should be pursuing." The researchers then present "anecdotal evidence" of the shortfalls of for-profit hospitals compared to not-for-profit and government hospitals.

SEVENTH

A study in 1986 by Renn, Schramm, Watt, and Derzon, according to The Fraser Institute, "found no significant difference in cost between for-profits and non-profits."

Many readers would come to a different conclusion after reading what the researchers themselves wrote. In their own words, the researchers summarize their findings this way:

> *[W]e found that investor-owned chain hospitals charged significantly more, and were more profitable, than all other types of hospitals except freestanding for-profits; there were no differences in productive efficiency that could be attributed to ownership or affiliation; the investor-owned hospitals had higher debt-to-asset ratios, less capital-intensive plants, and greater capital costs as a percentage of operating costs than the not-for-profits; and there were no consistent case-mix differences among the hospitals.*

In their conclusion, the researchers write: "Our results reinforce the theory advanced in prior research that, during the era of cost-based reimbursement and less sensitivity by private payers to the price of hospital care, investor-owned chain hospitals earned their higher profits by charging more rather than by costing less."

Eighth

The Fraser Institute report summarizes the findings of a study by Watt, Derzon, Renn, Schramm, Hahn, and Pillari (1986) in one sentence: "They discovered that adjusted costs per admission and per day were not significantly different between for-profit and non-profit hospitals."

In comparison, the researchers themselves say:

> *We found that total charges (adjusted for case mix) and net revenues per case were both significantly higher in the investor-owned chain hospitals, mainly because of higher charges for ancillary services; there were no significant differences between the two groups of hospitals in regard to patient-care costs per case (adjusted for case mix), but the investor-owned hospitals had significantly higher administrative overhead costs; investor-owned hospitals were more profitable; investor-owned hospitals had fewer employees per occupied bed but paid more per employee; investor-owned hospitals had funded more of their capital through debt and had significantly higher capital costs in proportion to their operating costs; and the two groups did not differ in patient mix....*

They then say, "We conclude that investor-owned chain hospitals generated higher profits through more aggressive pricing practices rather than operating efficiencies...." As with the study above, The Fraser Institute placed this study in its list of studies that "found no difference in performance" between for-profit and non-profit hospitals.

• • •

Rather than by evidence or successful examples, the drive to privatize Canada's medicare system is energized by an ideology committed to the virtues of market-based competition over co-operation; private gain over public wealth; and the rights, property, and welfare of the individual over the rights, property, and welfare of the community. Milton Friedman, the economist whose work is often used to justify this ideology, captured its spirit in these words, written almost 40 years ago:

Few trends could so thoroughly undermine the very foundations of our free society as the acceptance by corporate officials of a social responsibility other than to make as much money for their stockholders as possible. (Friedman, cited in Woolhandler and Himmelstein, 1999, p444)

Michael Walker, head of The Fraser Institute, uses different words: "I doubt there is a limit to the market way of thinking" (Todd). But an uncritical commitment to any ideology can lead people to the position that best fits the ideology, rather than the position supported by the best evidence. The valid evidence repeatedly confirms that health care is an example of market failure.

4
CREATING CRISIS

IT HAS OFTEN been said that Ralph Klein didn't become premier by running against the Liberal Opposition, but by running against his direct predecessor in the Progressive Conservatives, Don Getty. Don Getty became Premier of Alberta in October 1985, and stepped down in December 1992. Throughout the entire period of his government, the Province's spending on health care remained remarkably stable. In 1986, Getty's first full year in power, it was $1,360 per capita, and in 1992 it was $1,393 per capita, adjusting for inflation. In the years between it moved no more than $51 up or down, as Table One shows (Canadian Institute for Health Information, 1998, p108).

TABLE ONE
ALBERTA GOVERNMENT HEALTH EXPENDITURE
(per capita, constant 1986$)

1986	$1,360
1987	$1,330
1988	$1,333
1989	$1,386
1990	$1,411
1991	$1,366
1992	$1,393

SOURCE: CANADIAN INSTITUTE OF HEALTH INFORMATION

Keeping a tight rein on health spending was a constant management challenge for the Getty government, as it is for every government. Nurses struck for higher wages in 1988, doctors pressed for higher fees, and some hospitals closed beds. From 1990 to 1992 almost 1,000 nurses' jobs were eliminated across the province. But things could have been worse for the health sector. Spending in virtually every other public service—including education, social services, and transportation—was cut substantially.

Ralph Klein was a cabinet member in the Getty government from 1989 to 1992. He knew that strict constraints had been placed on spending for public programs. So did Jim Dinning, who also sat in Getty's cabinet, and who became Provincial Treasurer when Ralph Klein became Premier. The evidence was there in internal briefing documents, budget speeches in the Legislature, even a C.D. Howe Institute study (Taft).

Yet when he became Premier, Ralph Klein went into communications overdrive to convince Albertans that spending had been soaring in the Getty years. It is an astonishing and disturbing example of the power of a skilled and determined communicator to reshape information. Over and over, Premier Klein told Albertans that spending had been "out of control" before he came to power. There are countless examples. "When our new administration took over a year and a half ago…we saw uncontrolled spending," he told the newspapers in June 1994. In a speech to the Canadian Medical Colleges in April 1996, he declared, "In the 1980s, health costs in this province tripled" ("tripled" is underlined in his speech notes). A month later, after losing a byelection, he told the media his government was still "trying to get the cost of health care under control." On an open-line radio show that garnered front page coverage in newspapers, he told listeners, "We knew we had to get spending under control. We knew it was literally going through the roof" (Taft, pp 25, 64, 26, 25). Uncontrolled growth in public spending by previous governments was the story that served—and continues to serve—as the organizing myth of the Klein government. Without it, the central policies of his government seem incoherent.

Klein pounded away with this message. In a thirty-minute province-wide television address on 4 February 1997, he looked straight into the camera: "I want to spend a few moments on *health care*, because it's a top priority for Albertans and for our government. Four years ago, as part of our overall restructuring, we set out to reform health care. We had to. Costs were simply out of control." After describing some alarming—and distorted—statistics (see Appendix A), he repeated his message to the TV audience: "We had to get health care costs under control." As late as May 1999, he was still at it, telling the audience at an event in which the Fraser Institute gave Mr. Klein his third-straight Fraser Institute award for fiscal performance, that public program spending in Alberta was uncontrolled before he came to power (Mertl).

Those beneath Premier Klein in government followed suit. In a letter to the *Edmonton Journal* in March 1994, the Minister of Health, Shirley McClellan, wrote of "…health care costs doubling in Alberta in the last twelve years…." In truth, spending on health care by the Alberta government was $1,183 per person in 1982, and $1,208 in 1994, corrected for inflation (Canadian Institute for Health Information). In May 1995, the *Edmonton Journal* printed an article which prominently featured quotes from a government spokesman: "Up until 1993–94, health care costs had been rising about 12 to 13 percent each year for the last decade" (*Edmonton Journal*, 11 May 1995, pA7). In November 1996, Halvar Jonson, Shirley McClellan's replacement as Minister of Health, told the public that health-care spending had been "spiralling" (*Edmonton Journal*, 26 Nov. 1996, pA10; 8 Nov. 1996, pA6).

With a compliant media and a struggling opposition, this campaign based on misleading information succeeded. Inaccurate though the story was, the Government of Alberta under Ralph Klein convinced most of its own citizens that public spending on health care (and every other public service) was, in one of his terms, "skyrocketing," and had to be cut.

And cut they did. Provincial per capita spending on health care dropped 18 percent (after adjusting for inflation) in Klein's first full three years as premier, as shown in Table Two (Canadian Institute for Health Information, 1998, p108)

TABLE TWO
ALBERTA GOVERNMENT HEALTH EXPENDITURE
(per capita, constant 1986$)

1992	$1,393	
1993	$1,325	-4.9%
1994	$1,208	-8.8%
1995	$1,156	-4.3%

SOURCE: CANADIAN INSTITUTE OF HEALTH INFORMATION

The effects were dramatic. From 1992 to 1995, a total of 14,753 health-care workers in Alberta lost their jobs or had their positions reduced (Alberta Health, 1998). In the same period the Calgary Regional Health Authority and the Capital Health Authority in

Edmonton lost 4,400 staff. Lab services were reduced and privatized. Thousands of health-care jobs around the province were downgraded to part-time and lesser-skilled staff. Thousands of hospital beds were closed across the province (Taft). The results were predictably painful. Doctors, whom the Klein government had frozen out of decision-making regarding the cuts, became frustrated and upset, and there was a wildcat strike by hospital laundry workers in Calgary. In the winter of 1997, increasingly angry nurses nearly went on a province-wide strike. Waiting lists for services grew longer and became a frequent issue in the media. Public confidence in the health-care system eroded, and it became a political liability for a government that otherwise garnered voter support. (For more-detailed information on trends in health-care spending, see Appendices B and C.)

There was another fallacy built in to the story. Hospitals, schools, seniors, roads, and other public programs were blamed for something that wasn't particularly their fault: the growing provincial debt. "The problem is spending," Ralph Klein told the Edmonton Downtown Rotary Club, a month after becoming premier, "and the cause of that spending is a public that expects and demands more government than is needed." He then singled out health, education, and social services as areas of great concern (Taft, p62). He didn't tell his audience that spending in these areas had been curtailed for years, and that the fat had already been removed. The bigger culprits causing Alberta's fiscal problems were enormous private-sector subsidies, which consumed two to three billion dollars of Alberta's public wealth every single year from 1983 to 1990, a rate unrivalled in the rest of Canada (Taft, pp 112–113).

When these were combined with the collapse in Alberta's petroleum revenues after 1985, a massive provincial debt was inevitable. Health care and other public services were innocent bystanders caught in the crossfire—or perhaps, more accurately, scapegoats for a government trying to conceal its bad habits.

Ralph Klein's spending cuts left health care particularly disrupted in Calgary, the Premier's political home base. By 1996 the reductions had ended, and funding began to climb. But the sense of crisis did not lift. In much of the province, and particularly in Calgary, there were severe shortages of nurses, doctors, and other staff. Try as it might, the Calgary Regional Health Authority (CRHA) couldn't balance its books. Its deficit climbed. Despite Calgary's mushrooming population, the CRHA decided to shut down the Grace hospital and sell the Holy Cross hospital to for-profit investors, though the investors' intentions were not perfectly clear. Then, in October 1998, it took another dramatic step, demolishing the Bow Valley Centre (formerly the Calgary General) with a spectacular explosion.

A year after the blast, the new Chairman of the CRHA conceded Calgary would eventually need a new hospital, and the chief medical officer of the CRHA reaffirmed Calgary was seriously short of beds, nurses, and doctors (*Edmonton Journal*, 15 Dec. 1999, pA8). The Klein government announced substantial new funding for health care, but the details were confusing: in a personal editorial in the *Globe and Mail* on 3 December 1999, Mr. Klein wrote "Right now we are spending $800-million more annually on health than in 1993"; three days later in a personal editorial in the Canadian edition of *Time* magazine, he wrote, "Right now we are spending $545 million more annually on health than in 1993." The difference of $255 million was immense, but he offered no explanation for it.

In most regions of the province, the new funds meant public hospitals could consider re-opening wards they had mothballed or diverted to other uses (see Auditor General, 1999). But in Calgary, this option had been eliminated with the sale of the Holy Cross, the shutdown of the Grace, and the detonation of the Bow Valley Centre. Understandably, the public in Calgary was not impressed. The Klein government, having created this crisis, needed a solution. It still had two cards to play: first, replace the CRHA management, and second, privatize services. It would soon be time for another "public information" campaign.

5

THE BUSINESS

OF HEALTH CARE

IN CALGARY

EARLY IN ITS FIRST mandate the Klein government terminated the old system of hospital governance, with its huge number of boards and other organizations, and replaced it with 17 Regional Health Authorities (RHAs), plus province-wide cancer and mental-health boards. Each RHA had jurisdiction over the entire public health-care system—from vaccinations to nursing homes to teaching hospitals—in a designated area of the province. The RHAs' wide-ranging responsibilities for health were similar to those local school boards had for education. But there was one significant difference: RHA board members were not elected. They were appointed by the provincial cabinet and were accountable to the provincial government, not to citizens in their jurisdiction.

The Edmonton and Calgary RHAs dwarfed all others. They each included sophisticated teaching hospitals, renowned research programs, large populations and billion-dollar budgets. They were also quite different from each other. The Capital Health Authority in Edmonton was located in the only part of Alberta that rejected the Klein Tories and elected opposition MLAs in significant numbers instead. The Calgary Regional Health Authority (CRHA) was located in much friendlier territory. Calgary was the Klein Tories' urban power base, a strong nexus of government and corporate power that had wielded enormous influence over the entire province ever since Calgarian Peter Lougheed was elected Premier almost 30 years ago.

When Ralph Klein chose John (Bud) McCaig, an influential Calgary corporate leader, as the first chair of the Calgary Regional Health Authority (CRHA) in June, 1994, he sent a clear message: the private sector had the know-how needed to fix Alberta's "inefficient" and "costly" health-care system.

Mr. McCaig was the founder and CEO of Trimac Corporation, the largest bulk trucking company in North America. He was one of those entrepreneurs Calgarians like to brag about, someone who had built a business with his own sweat and then turned it into a corporate and financial powerhouse. He was also a part-owner of the Calgary Flames, and an influential Tory fundraiser (Braid). At the time of the appointment, Premier Klein was already well into his deficit and debt-slashing programs, a strategy that had been heartily endorsed by corporate Calgary. This was not Mr. McCaig's first alliance with the Klein government: Trimac is the majority owner of Bovar Inc., which operates the Swan Hills Hazardous Waste Disposal Treatment Plant. According to a report prepared by the Auditor General of Alberta, by 1994 Bovar had received upwards of $400 million in subsidies from the provincial government.

Bovar Inc., which at the time was 40 per cent owned by the Alberta government, had even managed to escape the Klein Tories edict of no more subsidies to business. Less than a week after Mr. Klein was elected Premier in

1993, cabinet secretly authorized a $100 million loan guarantee to Bovar (Alberta Hansard, 18 Oct. 1994).

This was not the only link to the Alberta government Mr. McCaig brought to his new position as chairman of the CRHA. As chairman of Trimac and Bovar Inc., Mr. McCaig was directly connected to a Bovar subsidiary, Bovar Biomedical Services. In 1992 Alberta Health ordered most Alberta hospitals to ship their waste to Bovar Biomedical's new incinerator in Beiseker, 50 kilometres north of Calgary. Three of the Calgary hospitals Mr. McCaig would oversee as Chairman of the CRHA already had contracts worth a total of $108,000 with one of his companies (Walker 1994). Mr. McCaig eventually resigned his position as chairman of Bovar and appointed his son Jeffrey.

And so a man who was directly connected to a company that had benefited from almost half a billion dollars of taxpayers' money was now charged with cutting about $140 million out of the Calgary region's $890 million health-care budget. But if Mr. McCaig was bothered by the irony, he didn't show it. He accepted his appointment and got down to the task of reorganizing and shrinking Calgary's health-care delivery system, just as Premier Klein had asked him to.

McCaig wasn't the only prominent Tory on the CRHA board. Norman "Skip" McDonald, president of Ralph Klein's constituency association, was also appointed. Then, in 1996 Bruce Libin, a lawyer and Tory fundraiser, was named to the board. Scobey Hartley, vice-president of communications for the Progressive Conservative Association of Alberta, is now on the board of the CRHA as well.

Under the guidance of Mr. McCaig, the CRHA board decided that the system would be more efficient and less costly if health services were concentrated in the city's newer hospitals: the Foothills, the Rockyview, the Peter Lougheed, and the Alberta Children's Hospital. The city's older hospitals—the Holy Cross (280 beds), the Grace (100 beds) and the old Calgary General, now called the Bow Valley Centre (450 beds, with a much larger capacity)—would be shut down. Even though Calgary's population was growing, there would be no inner city trauma or emergency wards, and no inner-city psychiatric facilities, and the bed closures would be permanent. The Foothills, which is linked to the University of Calgary's school of medicine and the Tom Baker Cancer Centre, was designated as the "head office" and soon became the administrative and resource centre of the Calgary system (Gold).

This industrial approach to health care efficiency appeared to be consistently supported by the 15 government appointees on the CRHA board. Like members of a corporate board they rarely disagreed in public. At their monthly public meetings they discussed only non-contentious issues, and did not allow questions or presentations from citizens in attendance.

Mr. McCaig didn't have to contend with much political opposition either. Most of the Calgary MLAs were Klein Tories. Calgary City Council decided that health care was no longer within their jurisdiction and for the most part remained neutral on the hospital closures. But there was intense pressure behind the scenes. Dr. Larry Bryan, the former president of Foothills Hospital and the first CEO of the new CRHA, quit after only eight months on the job. He said he was exhausted by the pace of required change and tired of political interference. "Politicians are doing their best to stand back. But they're under major pressure and their concerns come into this office on a pretty regular basis. This office is subject to a lot of political interest," he said shortly after announcing his resignation (Walker, 1995).

Most of the public opposition to the cuts and closures was voiced by doctors, who felt completely left out of the planning process, and by unionized CRHA employees who felt they were being slowly eased out of the health-care system altogether. In November 1995 the tension erupted into the streets, when laundry workers at the Bow Valley Centre called an illegal strike. The workers were angry that the hospital was contracting out laundry services only a year after they had agreed to take a 28 percent wage cut in favour of job security. Now they were to be laid off without severance. The illegal walkouts spread to other hospitals. Doctors and nurses voiced their support for the laundry workers, and before long Mr. McCaig and the CRHA had a full-scale uprising on their hands.

The provincial government eventually settled the dispute with a promise of more money for the region, but the illegal strike had managed to shed some light on one of the CRHA's first contracts with the private sector. The laundry contract had been awarded to K-Bro Linen Service Ltd., owned at the time by Edmonton's Kinasewich family (49 per cent) and Vencap Equities Alberta (39 per cent). Vencap was a venture capital fund partly owned by the Alberta government (30 per cent) until the government sold its interest to Onex Corporation in October 1995, about a month before the laundry workers walked off the job. Mr. McCaig had been on the board of Vencap until he resigned in May 1995 so his company, Trimac, could make a bid for Vencap. The bid collapsed in August, but if it had been successful Mr. McCaig's Trimac, through Vencap, would have had a 39 percent interest in K-Bro (Pedersen; *Alberta Hansard*, 25 Oct. 1995; Lisac; Sharpe and Bagnell; Pommer).

Early in his term as CRHA board chairman, Mr. McCaig had publicly supported the direct election of CRHA board members. But by 1997 he had changed his mind. "We're concerned about single issue people who might run with a view to reopening a hospital that has been closed, or any number of issues. They could be well-funded by a group, get their name on all the billboards, and we don't think that would serve the best interests of the community," he told the government's Standing Policy Committee on Health Planning (*Alberta Report*, 14 July 1997). Even though a government-appointed committee of MLAs had recommended electing two thirds of RHA board members, the government eventually quashed the proposal in favour of cabinet appointments.

By mid-1997 three of Calgary's eight hospitals had been emptied and closed. They were hulking monuments to the Klein government's fiscal agenda and constant reminders to Calgarians of the reasons for long waiting lists and crowded emergency wards. It was in this context that, in 1997, Mr. McCaig reached out to friends and acquaintances in the business community and convinced them to contribute a considerable amount of money for hospital equipment and medical research. Known as the "Partners in Health Initiative," the fundraising appeal was intended to ensure that the city's hospitals and medical school would continue to offer "world-class" health care, research and education. The campaign was chaired by Harley Hotchkiss, a well-known Calgary businessman and a part-owner of the Calgary Flames, and it raised $51.6 million from corporate and individual donors. Mr. McCaig, who is also a part-owner of the Flames, himself contributed more than $1 million, as did Alvin Libin, another Flames part-owner. At the time, Mr. Libin was also vice-president of Crownx Inc., a health-care and financial-service corporation whose subsidiaries included Extendicare Health Services Inc. The Seaman brothers—Doc, Don, and B.J—also contributed $1 million. The Seamans own a minority share of Bovar Inc.

Less than a year later, the Holy Cross Hospital was sold to private investors and the Bow Valley Centre was demolished. The dust and grit from the implosion of thousands of tonnes of bricks and mortar could be seen all over city. The slow motion collapse of the much-loved hospital was repeated on television newscasts across the country. For many people it became a symbol of the lengths to which the Klein government would go to carry out its agenda.

After presiding over deep cuts in the system, Mr. McCaig resigned as Chair of the CRHA before the demolition of the Bow Valley Centre, but strains and controversy continued to emerge. In the spring of 1999, the CRHA reported a $20 million deficit. But money wasn't the only thing the CRHA was short of: it needed more nurses, doctors and hospital beds to meet the needs of Calgary's population, which had grown by about 110,000 since the CRHA was established six years earlier.

According to the CRHA the city now needs 240 more family doctors to catch up with Edmonton's ratio of GPs to population. It is also having problems recruiting neurologists, psychiatrists, anesthetists, general surgeons and other specialists. Some beds have been added to acute care hospitals, but the total number

(1,786) is only slightly higher than the number of beds in 1994 (1,748). Quite simply, the cuts had gone too deep (Walker, *Calgary Herald*, 15 Dec. 1999; CRHA Backgrounder, 5 Dec. 1999).

The situation became so critical that when the provincial government brought down its budget in March 1999, the new CRHA Chairman, Dr. John Morgan, a retired cardiologist who had been in the position only a short time, said his region's funding allotment simply wasn't enough. Two weeks later a consultant's report commissioned by the CRHA board delivered a damning indictment. The firm of Watson Wyatt Worldwide interviewed 500 CRHA employees and doctors as well as MLAs. In its 14-page report it criticized the CRHA for its preoccupation with saving money, for its poor communication, for its excessive micro-management of hospital affairs, and for overloading the Foothills Hospital (Watson Wyatt Worldwide).

Within days, former provincial treasurer Jim Dinning was named CRHA Chairman. Over the next few months most CRHA board members and top executives were replaced.

6

JIM DINNING

PREPARES THE WAY

FOR PRIVATIZATION

LONG BEFORE LUNCH gets underway there are only a few empty chairs to be found among the 35 tables in the elegantly appointed ballroom of the Calgary Chamber of Commerce. Men and women in well-tailored suits shake hands, exchange business cards and chat enthusiastically with one another. Their name tags bear corporate identifications such as We Care, Extendicare, North American Medical Emergency Services (NAMES) and Health Resources Group (HRG) (Steward, 1999a).

They have paid 30 dollars (Chamber of Commerce members) or 45 dollars (non-members) to hear Jim Dinning give his first major speech, or to use his words "accountability session," since being appointed Chairman of the Calgary Regional Health Authority (CRHA) in April 1999, two months earlier.

Mr. Dinning, the former Provincial Treasurer, the man who planned and executed deep funding cuts to health care, education and social services five years earlier, was now a vice-president at TransAlta, the province's largest utility company.

The volunteer but very influential position put Dinning in charge of an organization that spends just over a billion public dollars a year, as much as the entire

Calgary municipal budget, and has 15,000 employees. Officially, Health and Wellness Minister Halvar Jonson had named Mr. Dinning as CRHA Chair. But it was no secret that Ralph Klein himself had called on Mr. Dinning, one of his most trusted lieutenants, to straighten out the CRHA, which was millions of dollars over budget and mired in controversy (Walker and Henton, *Calgary Herald*, 14 Apr. 1999). The two men had certainly worked well together when they were both in government. As Provincial Treasurer, Mr. Dinning presided over the detail required for a rapid elimination of the budget deficit, while Premier Klein used his considerable communication skills to sell the program to Albertans.

Amid the clatter of salad plates being set on tables, another trusted Klein lieutenant, Rod Love, can be seen glad-handing at tables near the front of the ballroom. Once the Premier's chief of staff and communications director, Love was given a communications contract with the CRHA at the same time Dinning was appointed. Gordon Olsen, director of Premier Klein's Calgary office, is also on hand, as is Barry Styles, a member of the Premier's "kitchen cabinet" and an advertising executive whose firm has large contracts with the Tory party and the provincial government. Several Tory MLAs and CRHA board appointees are also in attendance.

Premier Klein once referred to Mr. Dinning as the "Wayne Gretzky of Treasurers," and as the new chair of the CRHA stands to address the crowd he appears to be enjoying his regained fame. Nevertheless, he admits the CRHA has serious problems. A recent survey by Angus Reid found that two out of three Calgarians believe the CRHA is in a state of crisis. The biggest concern is access to care: one in four of those surveyed wants the CRHA to open more hospital beds. These results are no surprise to anyone, especially officials at the CRHA who have laid off hundreds of nurses, shut down two hospitals and blown up a third, while watching Calgary's population surge.

The CRHA depends on the Alberta government for funding and doesn't have much room in which to manoeuvre. As lunch is served, the CRHA already has a $20 million deficit, substantially more than any other RHA in the province, and it has been told not to expect any more money from provincial coffers even though the Alberta government has a large surplus.

But Mr. Dinning doesn't talk about overcrowded hospitals, long waiting lists or insufficient government funding. Instead, he says, "I intend to close the gap between the *perception* that there is a crisis and the fact that 84 per cent of people who use the system believe it works well." Mr. Dinning also assures the crowd that the CRHA has no intention of shelving new projects and that some day "a new hospital will have to be built in Calgary." The audience in the Chamber of Commerce ballroom applauds enthusiastically. Mr. Dinning then takes a few questions from the floor before ending his first "accountability session."

The following month Jack Davis leaves his post as chief civil servant of the provincial government and secretary to the provincial cabinet to become the new CEO of the CRHA. He too is a trusted Klein lieutenant.

• • •

Two months later, at the end of September 1999, an embarrassed Jim Dinning announced that the deficit at the CRHA had swollen from $20 million to $52 million.

He attributed the increase to an accounting glitch and Calgary's burgeoning population. In an editorial on 23 September 1999, the *Calgary Herald* defended the Klein-appointed trio of Dinning, Davis, and Love by claiming that they couldn't be expected to solve all the CRHA's problems overnight. The editorial then went on:

> *To his credit, Dinning has so far refused to compromise patient care to balance the books. Instead he's tried to find efficiencies, cut administration costs and increase revenue from parking and other user fees. But clearly that's not enough. And Dinning knows it.*
>
> *In recent public appearances, Dinning has talked about the need for deep-seated change, new ways of thinking and radical innovation. He has mused about whether health authorities need to narrow their mandates to do fewer things, but do them exceptionally well. And he has challenged MLAs to debate the role of private health care.*

Mr. Dinning's career had come full circle. He was the architect of the deficit elimination program that imposed severe funding cuts to public health care, cuts so severe that Dr. Larry Bryan, the first CEO of the CRHA, privately warned the government that it was cutting too much too fast. Bryan's advice was ignored and he left his post after only eight months (*Health Savvy*). Now Mr. Dinning, as chair of the CRHA, appeared to be the architect of measures to fix the damage.

Dinning's challenge to "debate the role of private health care" received a speedy reception: within several weeks Premier Ralph Klein bought TV time to announce he was undertaking a new approach to health care. He said his government was going to pass legislation to allow for-profit corporations to contract with regional health authorities to provide surgical services that—up until now—could only be provided by public hospitals, creating for-profit hospitals for the first time in Alberta's history.

The details of Premier Klein's plans were not clear and the legislation had not yet been drafted. But his position fit nicely with those of influential CRHA board members such as lawyer, venture capitalist, and Tory fundraiser Bruce Libin, who had been publicly advocating contracting out to the private sector (Walker, *Calgary Herald* 1 Feb. 1999 and 24 Mar. 1999). The announcement was also a shot in the arm for HRG, a group of business and medical professionals that had opened a surgical facility on the third floor of the former Grace Hospital in Calgary, and that had been lobbying to contract with the CRHA for hip-replacement surgery.

A few days later, Health and Wellness Minister Halvar Jonson announced additional health-care funding of $216 million. Almost 45 percent—$92.9 million—was destined for Calgary, including $40 million to wipe out the CRHA's deficit.

In early December 1999, Mr. Dinning held a Christmas party at his home for CHRA executives and board members. Among the guests? Ralph Klein. The team that had engineered such deep cuts to Calgary's and Alberta's health-care system—including Klein, Dinning, Love—was getting ready for a new year.

7

A GLIMPSE

INTO FOR-PROFIT

MEDICINE

PRIVATE, FOR-PROFIT hospitals and clinics are run by bright, hard-working, generously paid people who are well-trained and well-equipped. Why, then, do they so consistently fall short of the performance of their public counterparts? Managers and staff of both public and private health facilities face many of the same challenges: the complexities of caring for patients; the backroom politics of medical staff; nursing shortages; legal liabilities; new technologies; financial constraints; media snoops; committees; boards of directors; and on and on. But in for-profit facilities, administrators face relentless demands in addition to these—demands that take a lot of extra money, time, skill, and energy.

If the Klein proposals proceed, the Grace and Holy Cross hospitals in Calgary will be converted to for-profit facilities. Converting hospitals from non-profit to for-profit status was big business in the United States in the 1990s, creating "before-and-after" snapshots that offer a glimpse into why for-profit hospitals are costly and inefficient.

● ● ●

Michael Herbert led the successful conversion of a large US Health Maintenance Organization called Physicians' Health Services (PHS) from non-profit to for-profit status, and he has written about the experience. One immediate effect of the conversion, says Herbert, "…was that the demands on my time as chief executive officer increased about 30 percent, with a healthy chunk now necessarily being devoted to talking with existing investors, potential investors, and analysts. Also, PHS was now, as never before, subject to the infamous "tyranny of the quarterly earnings report" (Herbert, p123).

A year after becoming a for-profit organization, PHS faced a drop in earnings because of increased competition, bringing intense investor pressure on the company, as Herbert makes clear: "Here is the dilemma: Once you become a for-profit public entity and take on public equity capital…you cannot decide to reject the 'growth or go' imperative because your investors fully expect earnings growth of 15 percent or better, year after year" (p124).

PHS responded by developing a five-year plan. "Our primary conclusion as we developed our plan was that we had to 'grow or go,' and that meant betting the company on an expansion… We believed that this was the only way we could achieve the 30 percent or higher growth rate needed to sustain the growth in earnings to satisfy our investors." In short, the company had to get bigger fast if it were to pay the earnings expected by investors. PHS established three fundamental corporate goals: "…(1) to maximize the company's earnings; (2) to maximize growth; and (3) to become and remain a world-class organization" (pp 122–123). An important tool for PHS was stock options in the company: "[I]n the competition for the best human capital, PHS can offer stock options, which are invaluable in recruiting, retaining, and motivating key employees" (p123).

PHS did grow, often by buying competitors. Of course, while PHS was buying its competitors, some of them were trying to buy PHS, forcing it to fend them off. "We have invested substantial time and expense… constructing poison pill defences, putting in golden parachutes, fighting an expensive proxy fight, and meeting with investment bankers, lawyers, accountants, and other consultants" (p124).

PHS was a successful investment, as were for-profit HMOs throughout the United States. "With a 645 percent return on investment, public HMOs topped the list of all US industries, including computer companies, nursing homes, office supply companies, semi-conductor companies, and funeral service companies as the best place to have invested money between 1 January 1990 and 16 December 1994" (p122). Herbert was Vice-Chairman and co-CEO of PHS, and undoubtedly was paid top dollar and provided with stock options. He thought the conversion process a success, and from the perspective of shareholders it undoubtedly was. But it also illustrates some disadvantages inherent in for-profit medicine.

● ● ●

Burdens on management time

The demands on managers' schedules in major healthcare organizations are intense, whether the organization is for-profit or not-for-profit. But the nature of those demands is different in the for-profit sector, as Herbert found. In addition to all the complications of running a hospital, managers in the for-profit sector must spend a "healthy chunk" of their time devoted to investors, potential investors, and analysts, to the plotting of corporate take-overs and the construction of defences, to expensive proxy fights, to investment bankers, and to accountants, all of which Herbert notes. He doesn't mention the time and expense of preparing and implementing marketing plans, the costs of preparing share offerings and filing corporate reports, or the constant negotiations and transactions with insurance companies, to mention a few other demands. All of these require time and expensive expertise: the costs of executives, corporate lawyers, securities analysts, accountants, marketing consultants, and insurance specialists are immense in the for-profit health-care industry.

Thrust for profit and growth

Investors in for-profit health-care companies expect returns of 15 to 20 percent annually, and annual growth of 15 percent (Miller; Herbert). Investors squeeze managers to insure these profit and growth rates are achieved, creating the constant pressure to perform on quarterly earnings report. Creating profits and achieving growth are a condition of employment for managers of for-profit health facilities; failure means firing.

Michael Herbert's experience at PHS occurred in the US, but the demands for growth and profit are hitting the Canadian health-care system, too. Canadian health-care companies are paralleling American approaches. MDS, an Ontario-based company that bills itself as "an international health and life sciences" conglomerate, is associated with some of the largest health-care companies in the US. It has become a major player in medical-lab services in Alberta since the Klein government came to power. MDS is a major investor in—and is well represented on the board of—HRG, which wants to open an overnight surgical facility in Calgary. MDS describes itself this way in a recent "Investor Fact Sheet":

> *MDS has a strong record of growth and profitability. In 1998, the Company achieved its target of $1 billion in revenues two years ahead of schedule. MDS's stable, solid businesses generate strong cash flows that allow MDS to both invest in R and D [research and development] for internal growth and to acquire new businesses. A new target: $2 billion by 2003.*
>
> *MDS aims to double its revenues in five years while providing earnings per share growth at a compound rate of 15% over the same period…. MDS has achieved compound annual growth in both operating income and earnings per share over the past five years in excess of the 15% target established by the Company… MDS is organized…to make senior management of each sector accountable to Corporate management and the Board of Directors for the achievement of growth objectives.* (MDS "Investor Fact Sheet", January 2000)

The same thrust for profit and growth appears in investor documents produced by Gimbel Vision Inc. Their "Management Discussion and Analysis" for 18 May 1998, for example, says, "In 1997, revenues increased 130% [from 1996]…" because of opening new centres, and "a 39% increase in the number of procedures performed in established centres." According to this analysis, earnings before taxes and minority interest increased 58 percent from 1996 to 1997, and net earnings rose 27 percent. (Gimbel postings on SEDAR website, January 2000).

The profit levels required by health-care corporations appear in other ways, too. For example, the Alberta Workers' Compensation Board pays private surgical clinics to do various procedures, including orthopedic operations. The fees it pays include a 20 percent profit margin for the clinics, contributing to costs that are commonly two to four times higher than if the procedures were done in public facilities (*Edmonton Journal*, 29 Nov. 1999, pB1).

In remorselessly pursuing profit and growth, these companies are doing exactly what is expected of them. In many sectors of the economy the forces of competition, supply, demand, and price would constrain this drive. But as we will discuss below, health care is unlike most other sectors: in health care, competition, supply, demand, and price are extraordinarily open to distortion and manipulation. For any government wanting to constrain the forces of growth in its health-care budget, increasing the role of corporations dedicated to high growth rates is the height of folly. It lays the ground for financial disaster in health care.

Stock options and other incentives

Stock options and other incentives, as Herbert notes, are useful for getting key people to buy into the growth and profitability of for-profit health care. They give managers, clinicians, and others a vested interest in expansion and business success. By the mid-1990s, incentive bonuses averaged more than 40 percent of administrators' pay at for-profit hospitals in the US. Stock options can carry enormous value: when the CEO of the largest private hospital company in the US resigned in 1997 because of federal fraud investigations, he left with US$269 million in company stock (Woolhandler and Himmelstein, 1999).

Stock options are not the only type of special reward. For-profit hospitals and clinics can bolster demand for their services by offering incentives to physicians who send them patients. The incentives can be direct payments to the referring physician, or they can be less direct, including investment opportunities in the hospital or clinic, or other special arrangements. In the US, many states have laws prohibiting at least some of these practices, and there have therefore been many investigations into the for-profit health industry. In Canada, controls on these practices are less clear. For example, *Maclean's* magazine (1 June 1998) reported that private lab owners are known to "offer inducements [to physicians] for their business" that may include offering doctors free rent in lab-owned buildings, or paying inflated rents in buildings owned by doctors (cited in Fuller, 1999, p8).

Bonuses, stock options, and other incentives are costly, but from an investor's perspective they create powerful momentum for growth and profitability in a health-care organization. From other perspectives, they raise serious worries about cost control and medical practice. It has been long established that doctors are influenced by financial incentives in choosing the treatments they provide: doctors are attracted to treatments that offer the richest financial rewards (Hsiao; Gray,1997; Gratzer). Incentives such as stock options and paying physicians to send patients to a particular facility can generate unnecessary demands for services, pump up waiting lists, and drive up costs.

Organizational goals: business over health

The goals developed by PHS after it converted to for-profit status were, in the order PHS lists them:

1) maximize earnings;
2) maximize growth;
3) become a world-class organization.

Although PHS was in the health-care business, their goals do not mention "health," or "care," or "patient," or anything else relating to health care. Their goals could apply equally to a pizza company or an automobile manufacturer. In the for-profit health-care industry, providing health care is one means to the organization's goals, but not the only means. A canny take-over bid may add far more to share values than serving patients, and providing less rather than more patient care can improve profitability, as many Americans have learned to their dismay.

Compare the goals of PHS to those stated by the Alberta government. The mission of Alberta's Department of Health and Wellness is "to protect, maintain, restore and enhance the health of Albertans." Every regional health authority has the following goals set in legislation through The Regional Health Authority Act:

- *promote and protect the health of the population within the region and work to prevent disease and injury;*

- *assess, on an ongoing basis, the health needs of the region;*

- *determine priorities in providing health services in the region and allocate resources accordingly;*

- *ensure that reasonable access to quality health services is provided in and through the region;*
- *promote health services in a way that responds to the needs of individuals and communities, and supports the integration of services and facilities in the region;*
- *prepare and submit to the Minister of Health a proposal for a health plan for the region.*

Are the goals of for-profit medicine compatible with the goals of Alberta Health and Wellness, and the regional health authorities? In light of all the evidence, surely not. If the ophthalmology department of the Calgary Regional Health Authority, for example, listed as two of its major goals "maximizing surpluses" and "maximizing growth," they would almost certainly be rejected. Arnold Relman, a senior statesman of medicine in the US, puts the contrast between business goals and health-care goals plainly: "In business, success is measured in terms of increasing sales volume and revenues—the last thing we want to see in the health-care system" (p105).

Costly marketing

Like any business, the for-profit health-care industry must market itself. In Alberta, MRI (magnetic resonance imaging) clinics buy advertising on prime radio broadcasts, and eye clinics pay for newspaper advertising campaigns. The cost of marketing at private health facilities in Canada is difficult to estimate, but figures from the US show that it can be expensive. In 1992, the industry journal *Modern Healthcare* estimated one percent of total hospital expenditures was devoted to marketing; in 1994, the *New England Journal of Medicine* estimated that US$1.75 billion was spent on marketing private hospitals in the US; and in 1997, *Modern Healthcare* pegged the annual marketing budget of the largest US private-hospital chain at US$1,567 per bed. As well as boosting operating costs, marketing has other effects. It increases pressure on health services by stimulating demand (this, of course, is the purpose of marketing); it contributes to an effect called "the diseasing of society" in which healthy people are increasingly concerned they are unwell and need health services; and, experience in the US indicates it pressures non-profit hospitals into marketing of their own, to maintain public profile and credibility (*Modern Healthcare*, 1992, 22[5]:44, cited in Woolhandler, Himmelstein, and Lewontin; Woolhandler and Himmelstein [1997] p773; and *Modern Healthcare*, 1997:2, March 10, cited in Woolhandler and Himmelstein [1999] p446).

Financing inefficiencies

When Margaret Thatcher began her drive to bring market forces into the Britain's National Health System, she appointed as the head of her team of business advisors a corporate executive named Roy Griffiths, who among other things had served as legal advisor to Monsanto Chemicals. Griffiths examined Britain's health-care financing scheme, and soon came to a firm conclusion:

> *[We] should realize the enormous advantage we have in funding [health care] the way we do. That is, simplicity of administration over and above everything else. Once you start getting into insured schemes, the amount of paperwork is disastrous.* (May, p27)

Public health systems such as Britain's and Canada's can finance health care at a fraction of the administrative cost of private ones because they have a single system of accountants, computers, forms, and procedures, all focussed on delivering one plan. In contrast there are an estimated 1,500 major insurance providers in the US, with 1,500 sets of accountants, computers, forms, and procedures, each with many different plans (Rachlis and Kushner). The red tape is mind-boggling, and that is a big reason why the cost of administering Canada's health-care system is less than one-quarter the cost in the US. In a Canadian hospital, a small accounting department can track the budgets, handle the collections, and file the reports. In an American hospital the accounting departments are by comparison huge, dealing with a multitude of insurance schemes, individual payers, bad debts, and reports. A Canadian doctor can handle a month's billing in a few hours, tabulating the information and sending it by computer to the provincial billing service. An American doctor typically needs two full-time staff to handle the same functions, and chronically struggles with collections, appeals, and bad debts (Rachlis and Kushner). As Canadian doctors and clinics drift toward privatized care, they drift into administrative inefficiencies, bigger hassles, and higher costs.

Other costs of doing business: political contributions and taxes

For-profit health-care corporations need government funding to flourish. In Alberta, the pursuit of public money by the private health industry—whether from Regional Health Authorities, Alberta Health and Wellness, or agencies such as the Workers' Compensation Board—is a matter of basic business viability.

Even in the US, which has the most highly privatized health-care system in the world, more than half of total health-care expenditures now come from governments, and every major health-care corporation receives public funds. This requirement for taxpayer dollars encourages health-care corporations to cultivate strong ties to political parties. One way they do this is through political donations. Information from Alberta's Chief Electoral Office indicates that from 1994 to 1998, MDS, its affiliates and investors, contributed more than $46,000 to Alberta's Tories.

Finally, like other for-profit businesses, the private health industry pays taxes on property and income. While taxes add to the cost of private health-care services, they are not the root cause of its higher cost. At least two studies comparing for-profit and not-for-profit hospitals in the US found that even after eliminating the effect of taxes, for-profit hospitals were clearly more costly (Woolhandler and Himmelstein, 1997; Watt et al.).

The bottom line

Why does private health care cost more?

- Its fundamental purposes are to maximize growth and profitability.

- Investors expect returns of 15 percent annually.

- Investors expect growth of 15 percent annually.

- Executive teams, in addition to running health-care facilities, must devote substantial time and money to investor relations; marketing; corporate filings and securities requirements; and many other activities, many of which require expensive expertise.

- Stock options and other incentives add expense, and fuel a powerful vested interest among executives and clinicians that drives up service demand, revenues, and—in the process—costs.

- Marketing—research, design, implementation, evaluation—is both necessary and expensive.

- Processing the multitude of private insurance schemes requires far more administrative resources than are needed with the universal plans of a public system.

- Taxes on income and property must be paid, and political contributions become strategically useful.

None of these things are required of public health-care providers. So we shouldn't be surprised to learn that research consistently finds for-profit health-care organizations more expensive than their public counterparts, and clearly shows hospitals that convert to for-profit status see their costs jump. Nor should we be surprised to read that highly regarded journals, after examining decades of evidence, publish statements such as, "[F]or-profit hospital ownership itself contributes to higher per capita costs…"; "[b]usiness strategies unrelated or even detrimental to efficiency can bolster profitability and market share…"; and "…market medicine is a failure…" (in order: Silverman, Skinner, and Fisher, p425; Woolhandler and Himmelstein, 1997, p774; Himmelstein, David U., et al, p163).

But all businesses face the costs discussed in this chapter, and market forces—competition, supply, demand—usually maintain an acceptable balance between supplier and consumer. What's so different about health care? More about that in Chapter 9.

8

HRG: THE EDGE

OF THE WEDGE

CALGARY'S GRACE HOSPITAL looks like an ordinary, three-storey, red-brick building from the outside. It no longer bears the name Grace as it did when it was a thriving and much-loved maternity hospital owned by the Salvation Army and an integral part of Calgary's public hospital network. Now it is simply labelled Health Resource Centre, and passers-by are more likely to see construction workers than mothers with their new-borns.

It looks ordinary, but ever since the Calgary Regional Health Authority (CRHA) decided it couldn't afford to fund the Grace and shut it out of the city's public health-care system, it has become a battleground. Inside is Health Resources Group (HRG), a group of Calgary business and medical professionals who seek contracts for services that would make the old building Alberta's first privately owned, for-profit, acute care hospital. Arrayed around them are various community, medical, union, business and political organizations determined to stop them.

HRG was incorporated in 1996, and it soon after made arrangements to lease the third floor of the recently closed hospital from the Salvation Army. After undertaking extensive renovations that included top-of-the line surgical suites and post-operative recovery rooms, HRG began working and lobbying to be certified to provide overnight surgery. But each time it sought to move the boundaries of the health-care system to include what most observers would describe as private-sector, for-profit hospitals, HRG's initiatives aroused stiff opposition from the public. By the fall of 1999, HRG backers had invested $10 million in their project, but it seemed stalled (Geddes).

They had failed to convince the public and much of the medical community of the need for a privately owned hospital that would operate outside the public health-care system, so in 1999 they changed their strategy and began lobbying for publicly funded contracts. Then, in November 1999, Premier Klein announced his plans to introduce legislation allowing private companies to contract with regional health authorities for overnight surgical procedures, such as hip replacements. This was exactly what HRG had pursued: the right to own and run a facility providing acute-care services under contract to the CRHA. Now they had Premier Klein on their side. What more could they ask?

The investors

Right from the beginning, HRG has been owned by a mix of local investors and larger corporate interests. The most familiar face among them is Frank King. The former oil-company executive became famous in Calgary during the 1980s when he chaired the 1988 Winter Olympics Organizing Committee. Another HRG director, Calgary architect Peter Burgener, was once president of the Alberta Association of Architects and is married to Jocelyn Burgener, Tory MLA for Calgary Currie. William Cochrane, formerly dean of medicine and president at the University of Calgary, had been an assistant deputy minister in the Alberta government in the 1970s and later became CEO of

Connaught Laboratories, one of Canada's premier biotech companies.

HRG directors also include Dr. Steve Miller, chief of orthopedic surgery at Calgary's Foothills Hospital, and an associate clinical professor at the University of Calgary.

In 1997, HRG recruited Jim Saunders, chief operating officer for the CRHA, to become HRG's executive director and chief spokesman (HRG, 1997). Saunders knew the landscape of Calgary's health-care system inside out. He had held executive positions in several Calgary hospitals, and while he was chief operating officer of the CRHA, the authority had decided to close the Grace and Holy Cross hospitals, and the Bow Valley Centre.

While the local investors in HRG give the consortium a Calgary face, the relationships of some directors with other ventures link HRG to several large corporations. Dr. Miller, the orthopedic surgeon, is also chief medical officer for Columbia Health Care Inc., a privately held rehabilitation company with 33 centres across Canada. Columbia was at one stage wholly owned by the Sun Healthcare Group, based in New Mexico, which operates rehabilitation clinics and nursing homes (Statistics Canada). Sun sold Columbia after financial difficulties.

Another HRG director, Tom Saunders (no relation to Jim Saunders), was vice president of Sun's Canadian operations until the sale of Columbia. Mr. Saunders and Dr. Miller founded Western Occupational Rehabilitation Centre, which was later sold to Columbia Health Care Inc.

Dr. Cochrane, the former dean of the University of Calgary medical school, is the Alberta representative for

MDS Health Ventures, a venture capital investment fund which is 38 percent owned by MDS Inc. MDS Inc., mentioned in Chapter 7, is a large, Toronto-based medical services corporation listed on the Toronto Stock Exchange: its 1998 Annual Report shows that it had revenues of just over $1 billion that year. Richard Lockie, who heads up the Ontario arm of MDS Health Ventures, is also an active member of the HRG board. Mr. Lockie is senior vice-president of MDS Capital Corp., which is 37 percent owned by MDS Inc. Through the Canadian Medical Discoveries Fund where Mr. Lockie is chief financial officer, MDS Capital Corp. has invested $2 million in HRG (Canadian Medical Discoveries Fund Inc., 1999 Annual Report).

MDS Inc. earns much of its money from diagnostic laboratories billing to the governments of Ontario, Alberta, and British Columbia. In Calgary, a partnership of MDS-Kasper Medical Laboratories and 703590 Alberta Inc., a wholly owned subsidiary of the CRHA, has had a long-term contract since 1996 to manage and operate all diagnostic laboratories in Calgary. In 1999 alone, the CRHA paid $88 million to the joint venture for lab services (CRHA Backgrounder). MDS Inc. also has sizeable contracts with large health-care corporations in the US.

Crown Life Insurance of Regina, wholly owned by Canada Life Financial Corporation, has also invested in HRG. Ken Selinger, a bond and equity fund manager for Crown Life, confirmed that he attends HRG board meetings, although he is not named as a director or shareholder in HRG's corporate registration documents. He declined in an interview to reveal the exact amount of Crown Life's investment in HRG.

There is another Calgary connection to Crown Life. Alvin G. Libin, a prominent Calgary businessman and former chairman of the Foothills hospital, was a director of Crown Life from 1984 until May 1999, by which time the company had been acquired by Canada Life. Mr. Libin is also a long-serving director of Extendicare Inc., one of the largest operators of long-term care facilities in North America. Extendicare owns three facilities in Calgary that have contracts with the CRHA (CRHA, 1998). Mr. Libin is also a former chairman of the Alberta Heritage Foundation for Medical Research, a funding body established by the Alberta government. Bruce Libin, mentioned above as a member of the CRHA board, is Alvin Libin's nephew.

Iain Harris, chairman and chief executive officer of Summit Holdings Ltd., a private holding and investment company based in Vancouver, is also a member of HRG's board. Mr. Harris was president and chief executive officer of AirBC between 1983 and 1995. Prior to that he was vice president of finance and administration for the Jim Pattison Group, one of the largest privately-held companies in Canada (Financial Post Appointment Notice, June 18, 1998).

Protecting the investment

HRG operates on the third floor of the former Grace Hospital. Its services include 37 medical/surgical/rehabilitation beds (including four ICU beds), eight day-surgery beds, six recovery beds, three operating rooms, x-ray equipment, and laboratory services (HRG, 1997).

Often described as a cross between a first-class medical facility and a four-star hotel, HRG proposed to fill its beds and operating theatres with clients referred by the Alberta Workers' Compensation Board (WCB) and other third-party purchasers of health care (HRG Health Resource Group, *A Plan for the Organization and Delivery of Complementary Health Care in Canada*, 1997). HRG had planned to contract with the WCB for surgical services on the grounds that WCB would have to pay less to injured workers if they could get them into and out of hospital faster. But if their proposal was to be successful, HRG needed certification to operate as an overnight facility offering hospital services outside the public health-care system. It would be the edge of the wedge.

While the provincial government and the CRHA didn't express support for the idea, they didn't oppose it either. Instead, the government asked the College of Physicians and Surgeons to evaluate the facility's application for certification. The College declined to make a recommendation, so the hot potato was tossed back to the provincial government. In the spring of 1998, Halvar Jonson introduced Bill 37, which would have given him the power to approve private hospitals. But there was so much public opposition to the bill the government eventually withdrew it. HRG worked to secure more contracts from third parties, turning to the RCMP, Aboriginal Affairs, and the armed forces. But many of HRG's beds and surgical suites stayed empty. Management documents show that for the year ended 31 March 1999, revenue was $566,000 less than budget due to lower-than-anticipated bed nights and surgery hours. During the same period, operating expenditures exceeded budget by $29,000. One unexpected expense—legal fees and communications related to Bill 37—accounted for $56,000. HRG's net loss for 1998–1999 totalled $2.1 million, $726,056 more than anticipated (HRG, 1999a). By the end of 1999, the original $10 million invested in HRG had dwindled to $6 million (Geddes).

In the spring of 1999, directors decided to lobby aggressively for contracts with the CRHA. At the 25 March 1999 board meeting three approaches were agreed upon, as the following excerpt from documents in our possession labelled as minutes of the meeting show:

- *Enter a contract with the CRHA. Orthopedic surgeons initiate and forward a letter to the CRHA outlining reasons why CRHA should contract to HRG...*

- *Enter into other contracts (ie; podiatry, gastroplasty, etc.)*

- *HRG board members to review the key contact lists of CRHA, CPSA (College of Physicians and Surgeons of Alberta) and Calgary caucus and begin aggressively lobbying each of the lists.* (HRG, 1999b)

At HRG's 30 April 1999 board meeting held by teleconference, there was discussion of plans for an "ortho tower." According to documents labelled minutes of that meeting:

HRG met with 25 orthopedic surgeons on April 14th. Cy Frank and Doug Smith are proceeding with a draft proposal to the CRHA to do a pilot project at HRC [Health Resources Centre, the former Grace hospital]. The first draft will be complete by May 10th for HRG's review and input. The proposal will then be submitted to CRHA by May 15, 1999. (HRG, 1999c)

Dr Cy Frank is the chief of orthopedics for the CRHA. He is also on staff at the McCaig Centre for Joint Injury and Arthritis Research located at the University of Calgary. When contacted by phone Dr. Frank said he had not been involved in the preparation of HRG's proposal to the CRHA. "That would have been their hope, not the reality," he said. In November 1999 a CRHA physicians' task force concluded several options were available to clear the backlog for joint surgery. The options included contracting with HRG to provide surgical services or aftercare (Walker, *Calgary Herald*, 1 Dec. 1999).

The documents labelled 30 April 1999 also state: "A meeting needs to be scheduled with HRG and Jim Dinning, new Board Chair of the CRHA re: community clinics."

Even with these extra efforts, HRG's problems continued. Two of their early investors, Jim Viccars and Nigel Patchett, broke from HRG to set up their own company, Healthchoice Corp. In October 1999, Healthchoice tendered a $9 million offer to the Salvation Army to buy the Grace. The Salvation Army accepted and HRG found itself leasing space from Healthchoice Corp. Healthchoice announced that it wanted to convert the three-storey building into a long-term care facility and lease extra space to acupuncturists, massage therapists, and other practitioners who would offer a blend of traditional and alternative medicine (Steward, 1999c). Without the possibility of controlling the entire hospital, HRG's prospects looked gloomy. But when Premier Klein told Albertans in his television address that new private facilities would soon be a reality in Alberta, HRG investors had reason to smile again.

The former Grace Hospital had become divided territory. On the third floor, HRG continued with day surgery and looked forward to the time when it could finally begin offering surgery that required overnight stays. On the second floor, Healthchoice undertook extensive renovations to the old maternity hospital. It had already secured a contract with the CRHA to provide 34 long-term-care beds and was doing everything it could to make sure the old hospital stayed in its hands. When Healthchoice was unable to raise the money it needed to close the deal with the Salvation Army at the end of November, it looked as though HRG would emerge the victor at the old Grace. But the Salvation Army extended the conditional sale until the end of January 2000, and then to 15 February 2000, so as we complete this book, the future of the old Grace remains unresolved. The distractions of for-profit medicine were already a reality in Alberta.

9
THE OUTER LIMITS

EVERY INDUSTRY spends money on marketing, pays returns to investors, strives for growth, pays taxes, and offers stock options and bonuses to key figures. So why do these practices create special problems in health care? Why do market forces generally drive efficiencies up and costs down in most industries, but drive efficiencies down and costs up in the health industry? Economic theory explains why market forces are tremendously productive with many products. It also recognizes that free markets are not well-suited to everything. In fact, *the very principles that explain why private for-profit economics work well for computers and fast food, explain why they don't work well with health care.* Health care represents one of the outer limits of the marketplace.

Normal market processes work well when several basic conditions are met:

- There need to be lots of sellers and lots of buyers, so no one can single-handedly influence the price or supply.

- Sellers and buyers need to be easily able to enter and leave the market.

- Buyers must be knowledgeable enough to make informed decisions.

- Products must be standardized, so that buyers are as happy to buy from one seller as from any other.

- Prices must be free to go up and down without interference.

- Customers must be able to substitute one product for another (for example, hamburgers for pizza, or one radio station for another) (Fellows et al; Gray 1986b; Rice).

Where the conditions of a free market are generally met, economic theory predicts that for-profit competition will work well enough that a low level of government involvement will be needed. Plenty of evidence supports this theory. For instance, with fast foods the basic requirements for a successful market are met, so—as economic theory predicts—prices are reasonable, there are no shortages, customers are generally satisfied, and the most efficient makers of the tastiest foods flourish. A minimum of government involvement is needed.

But fast-food economics don't work in health care, and even champions of free markets recognize this. Alain Enthoven (the guru of internal market reforms in Britain's NHS) and Mark Pauly (an American health economist who favours some role for market forces in health care) openly recognize the necessity of major public intervention in health care to compensate for the failures of the market (Peterson; Pauly). And paradoxically, after arguing at length that health care is a market commodity much like food, David Gratzer backs away from advocating a free market in health care, instead proposing that Canada develop a system of medical savings accounts. But if health care is a normal commodity why do we need medical savings accounts when we don't need "food savings accounts" or "clothing savings accounts"? A handful of crucial reasons explain why market forces do not work well in health care.

The imbalance of knowledge

Society furnishes years of intense education to some of its brightest minds to train them as physicians, which is exactly why patients seek them out and value them. This expertise gives physicians tremendous influence over patients, who are generally not in a position to make well-informed diagnoses, interpret test results, or undertake clinical procedures. It is one thing to judge a slice of pizza; it is quite another to judge a course of medication, the reason for a painful hip, or the cause of a severe headache. And in addition to having more knowledge than patients, the physician usually has another advantage: he or she is not sick.

The former editor-in-chief of the *New England Journal of Medicine*, Dr. Arnold Relman, has described how these factors affect the doctor-patient relationship:

> *Unlike the independent shoppers envisioned by market theory, sick and worried patients cannot adequately look after their own interests, nor do they usually want to. Personal medical service does not come in standardized packages and in different grades for the consumer's comparison and selection. Moreover, a sick patient often does not have the option of deferring his purchase of medical care or shopping around for the best buy.* (Relman, p100)

Access to the health-care system

Doctors have another crucial advantage over patients: they control access to drugs, tests, specialists, and hospitals. When it comes to using the health-care system, patients depend on—and in many ways are under the direct control of—doctors. Patients can't write their own prescriptions or refer themselves to specialists, nor can they admit themselves to hospitals. There are good reasons for these controls: public safety with drugs, cost controls on unnecessary tests, assuring that hospital beds are available for those who need them most. As the gatekeepers of the health-care system, doctors serve as patient advisors and advocates, representing the best interests of the patient to the health-care system. In this position, the doctor is both a supplier of services to the patient and a demander of service from the system, operating, as Fellows et al. say, "on both sides of the market." (pp 167–168). This requires from doctors a morality of service rather than self-interest. We don't want doctors "selling" their patients to whatever lab, hospital, or surgeon bids the highest prices—we want doctors doing what's best for patients.

Difficulties with "shopping around"

The competitive forces that give consumers real power in free markets do not—and probably cannot—work well in health care. Shoppers can test drive cars, try on a new suit, or walk through show homes; they can return products for refunds; they can get repairs made under warranties. But how can a patient "test drive" a cancer therapy? A patient can't "return" an unsatisfactory eye operation. People with pains in their chests or with children running high fevers are not at the same liberty to "comparison shop" as someone looking for a new refrigerator. On top of this, many health-care services are not presented in standardized forms that allow for ready comparison, and it is not easy to substitute products; a knee replacement does not substitute for a hip replacement in the way a rack of lamb substitutes for roast beef, or a minivan substitutes for a sedan.

The necessity of trust

People who are vulnerable through a lower level of expertise, or because of illness, frailty, or fear for themselves or their loved ones, should be able to trust that their vulnerability will not be exploited. Few patients want to distrust their doctors, or to always question whether their doctors' advice is intended to benefit the patients or the doctors' bank balances. The doctor-patient relationship depends on trust.

In a strictly commercial market, sellers try to induce customers to buy. Sellers and buyers are each assumed to place their own interests above all others. The fundamental ethic is "buyer beware," and everyone must fend for themselves. This is not just the reality of the marketplace, this is its ideal. The theoretically perfect market is based on relentless self-interest.

Contrast this to the ideal doctor-patient relationship. Throughout history, society has expected physicians to act in the best interests of their patients, placing care and compassion above profit. The International Code of the World Medical Organization says, "[A] doctor must practice in his profession uninfluenced by motives of profit" (Relman, p99). The Canadian Medical Association Code of Ethics begins, "1. Consider first the well-being of the patient. 2. Treat all patients with respect; do not exploit them for personal advantage." The highest aspiration of the medical profession has always been, says Relman, "to serve the needs of the sick" (p100).

In return for this commitment, society grants physicians important benefits, including: a claim on a generous income; high status and a title; a licensed monopoly to practice; the right as a profession to self-regulation; and access at public expense to hospitals and equipment needed to treat patients, offsetting overhead costs that ordinary businesses must face.

The ideal of trust is not always achieved, and in fact there is widespread and well-documented evidence that doctors are influenced in their patient-care decisions by the opportunity to increase their incomes. Various studies have clearly linked changes in the rates of tonsillectomies, hysterectomies, coronary bypass procedures, and other medical procedures to changes in the amounts doctors are paid for them, with the numbers of procedures rising and falling not as patient needs rise and fall, but as the prices paid to physicians rise and fall (see for examples Hsiao; Gratzer; Rachlis and Kushner). This pattern reveals an often-noted flaw in the fee-for-service payment system, the so-called "perverse incentive" to over-serve patients, which drives up health-care costs and can threaten patient health more than improve it.

Proponents of for-profit health care argue that the problems of fee-for-service medicine can be overcome by introducing more market forces. In essence, health care should move away from the traditional ideal of trust, toward the market ideal of "productive self-interest." But given that the market works through financial incentives and self-interest, increasing market forces seems likely to worsen the influence of money and self-interest on patient-care decisions, and to erode the trust enjoyed by doctors, clinics, and hospitals.

Researchers have found that the incentives used for physicians in for-profit HMOs in the US significantly affect physicians' patient-care decisions, while those used in non-profit HMOs do not. In another study (unpublished), Florida officials found that the length of time patients with a given illness spend in hospitals varies dramatically according to whether the physician had a financial stake in the hospital. If the physician had an ownership position in the hospital, patients stayed an average 8.48 days, while if the physician did not have an ownership stake, the patient stayed 13.5 days. The officials were concerned because the payments to the hospitals were the same for all patients. The study concluded that the physicians were either sending their sickest patients to the hospitals they did not own, or they were treating the patients they sent to their own hospitals differently. Finally, indicators in the US ranging from "disenrolment rates" at for-profit HMOs, to the number of appeals filed by patients, to a large survey of patients, suggest that "trustworthiness problems grow in concert with the growth of investor control of health care organizations" (Gray 1997, p38).

Overbuilt capacity and inefficiencies

If health care lent itself to normal market forces, too much capacity—hospitals, clinics, equipment—would drive prices down and force inefficient facilities to close, at least in the private sector. But researchers consistently uncover the puzzling situation that clinics, hospitals, and equipment are higher priced and less efficiently used in for-profit medicine than in public medicine, and yet the for-profit sector flourishes. For-profit American hospitals often run 30 to 40 percent below capacity, lower than their public counterparts (Relman), and much lower than Canadian hospitals. Far more equipment is installed in each hospital than is justified or efficient. One report on this issue says, "[H]ospitals are rushing to purchase \$3 million 'gamma knives,' which are used for very rare neurosurgery. By some estimates, only six of these high-tech machines are needed for all the US, yet there are already two in Coral Gables, Florida" (Wiener, p121). For-profit clinics invest in new MRIs, while existing ones at other clinics are not fully booked. As another example, after a decade of experimenting with market forces, "…Singapore is saddled with widespread duplication of expensive medical equipment and high-technology services" (Hsiao, p264).

As mentioned above, some evidence shows that private hospitals offer competitive prices on services such as room rates, and then charge high rates for services such as drugs and lab work. Other evidence shows that for-profit clinics and hospitals compete by offering the fanciest technology and the most-famous doctors instead of reducing prices and improving efficiencies. A "star system" develops among doctors, with private hospitals paying huge amounts to attract doctors who will draw patients, driving up all doctors' salaries in the process. In a good example of the topsy-turvy economics of for-profit health care, a 1993 study of administrative costs in 6400 US hospitals found that as the number of patients declined, the number of employees increased to struggle ever harder for more market share and to squeeze more from insurers (Watt et al; Evans, 1997; Hsiao; Rice; Woolhandler, Himmelstein, and Lewontin).

These strange economics occur because consumers are not generally able to make well-informed decisions, the forces of competition are weak, and the doctor-patient (or supplier-consumer) relationship arises from trust rather than self-interest. In these circumstances, it is easy to over-sell services, maintain high prices, disguise inefficiencies, and boost profits. In systems where this is the norm, everyone pays the price, because the costs pass on to consumers through bigger insurance premiums and higher taxes to fund health care.

Increased regulation

On top of all these problems, when market forces are introduced in a sector to which they are not well-suited, there is typically a need for more rather than less regulation. This paradox is painfully evident in a mixed system of health care, as the British discovered when they introduced market reforms in the NHS: "Unleashing the wile and power of everyone looking out for his or her own interests is so dangerous in medicine, and there are so many ways not to compete on price or efficiency, that rules upon rules have to be written and enforced" (Light, p167). The costs of developing and implementing contracts, rules, and other aspects of an internal market system were so great in Britain that even market advocates questioned whether the results were worth it (Blomquist, 1995). An ethic of well-deserved trust offers an easily forgotten advantage over the "buyer beware" ethic of the market: "[T]rust is very efficient, and distrust is very costly" (Light, p167).

● ● ●

Market failure

Taken together, the factors discussed above disqualify health care as a commodity suited to being regulated by market forces. In the jargon of economics, health care is widely regarded as a market failure, and despite countless efforts by market enthusiasts to frame a case arguing the opposite, this has never changed.

One startling indicator of this market failure is that by 1994 in the United States, where market influences in health care are stronger than anywhere else, *public-sector spending alone* on health care was US$1,599 per capita, for a system in which 37 to 41 million people have no health-care insurance, and most other people or their employers face substantial deductibles, fees, and premiums (Thorpe). By contrast, in Canada, public-sector spending was US$150 less—US$1,444—for a system that offers universal first-dollar coverage for hospital and medical care. "Americans thus pay more *in taxes* for health care [than Canadians or almost all other people in the developed world] in addition to (or despite) their massive contributions through the private sector" (emphasis in original, Evans 1997, p459). Even experiments with limited market forces—internal markets, medical savings accounts, contracting out clinical services—appear to increase costs and inefficiencies far more often than they reduce them.

The shift away from a service ethic towards a commercial ethic, says an evaluation of Britain's market reforms written by a health economist from the United States,

> ...*is perhaps the most profound and costly danger for any health care system... [R]eformers have been quite naive about what competition unleashes; it teaches clinicians and managers to maximize profits and gains for themselves. The invisible hand of the market is said to transpose such behaviour into maximum value, innovation, efficiency, and responsiveness. But the clinicians and managers learn quickly to look out for themselves by competing in ways that drive costs up.* (Light, p166)

Advocates of for-profit medicine such as Gratzer argue that medicare "corrupts" the doctor-patient relationship by exempting it from market forces. But economic theory and the evidence both demonstrate that it is market forces that corrupt both the doctor-patient relationship and the safe and efficient functioning of a health-care system.

10

THE

ENTREPRENEURIAL

DOCTORS

ARE THEY DOCTORS first or businessmen first? That's been the key question ever since Dr. Howard Gimbel established the first off-hospital eye surgery site in Canada in Calgary in 1984. A well-respected ophthalmologist, Dr. Gimbel believed that with advanced technology he could perform more eye surgeries, such as cataract removal, if he moved into a private clinic setting rather than continuing to work at public hospitals. He became the first surgeon in Canada to use ultrasound to remove cataracts, the first to use a laser to correct astigmatism (Nelson).

By 1994, demand for his procedures was so intense that Alberta Health was paying a total of $9 million to Dr. Gimbel's clinics (Gray, Charlotte). Surgeons at the Gimbel clinics billed Alberta Health for their work, at about $550 per cataract operation. Dr. Gimbel also charged patients a "facility fee" of up to $1,200 which they paid out of their own pockets. It was meant to cover disposable equipment, nurses, and other over-heads—costs for which hospitals receive provincial funding. "I don't think we should be denying Canadians the right to spend their disposable income that they might have to spend on hockey games or a vacation or something, to spend it on something in regard to their health. I don't think that threatens the system," the eye specialist was once quoted as saying (Nagle).

The Klein government didn't have a problem with the way the Gimbel Clinics used public money to build a business and then charged extra fees to build in a profit. The Klein government was so supportive of Dr.Gimbel's enterprise that, when levied $3.6 million in fines by the federal government for contravening the Canada Health Act's ban against extra-billing, the Alberta government chose to pay the fine rather than tell Dr. Gimbel to stop charging facility fees. Then it agreed to cover facility fees.

But the 1996 resolution of the extra-billing dispute opened the door for even more private clinics. For instead of banning extra-billing, the Klein government now covered the surgical procedure *and* the facility fee charged by private clinics. "This forward-looking plan reflects a commendable response to the changes occurring in the delivery of health care, specifically surgical services," said Dr. Gimbel, who by then was running the biggest private medical clinic in Canada (Walker, 1996). Many Calgary doctors feared the new policy would undermine hospital emergency departments, teaching, and other public programs because so much money would be sucked out of the public system and channelled into private clinics. Others planned to upgrade and expand their private clinics.

At first, Bud McCaig, chair of the Calgary Regional Health Authority, also opposed the government's plan on the grounds that it would create too much demand for eye surgery, and that the CRHA didn't have enough funds to foot the bill. But only two months later, the CRHA announced that all eye surgery would be moved out of the hospitals and invited eye specialists to bid for the work. At the same time, the CRHA placed a cap on the amount of money to be spent annually on insured eye surgery.

Today Dr. Gimbel's Calgary clinics are part of Gimbel Vision International Inc. The company is listed on the Toronto Stock Exchange and has expanded into other parts of Canada, the US, Brazil and China. It was ranked as the fourteenth fastest-growing company in Alberta between 1995 and 1997, with a 469 percent increase in revenue and a 100 per cent increase in pre-tax profit (Nelson). In 1998, annual revenue grew to $20.8 million from $14.9 million in 1997 as earnings grew from $1 million to $2.3 million.

With results like that, it's not surprising that other Calgary doctors look to the "Gimbel-style" private clinic as a way of making more money than is possible through the ordinary system of payments from Alberta Health Care. Such clinics can offer both insured procedures, such as cataract surgery, and uninsured procedures, such as laser treatment for near-sightedness, as well as enhancements and extras. Private clinics also allow some independence from large, bureaucratic hospitals. Patients see the private clinic as a way of getting what they want faster than the public system can provide it.

The "eye business" has boomed in Calgary. Billboard advertising by various clinics dots the city. Competition between clinics has driven down the price of uninsured procedures. But to make up for the discounts, the clinics have had to increase patient load. "My whole perception of that industry is that there is so much price competition that the volumes have to really soar to maintain the bottom line," said Alf Sailer, an analyst with Calgary's Acumen Capital Partners. "What we're seeing is that routine laser surgery that recently cost $2,500 to $3,000 an eye, even Gimbel is now doing for $1,500.... And another group [Lasik Vision Corp.] is offering two-for-one specials..." (Nelson).

The result of the intensified competition is exactly what most health economists would predict: although they have the most eye surgeons in Alberta, Calgarians face the longest waiting lists and the highest fees for cataract surgery. The over-investment in high-tech equipment, along with expenses such as marketing, are costs that must be picked up by the consumer (or the taxpayer): despite the "price wars", the price of cataract surgery in Calgary is higher than anywhere else in the province. At the same time, the waiting lists are longest—at least for those seeking surgery under medicare—because the clinics are under pressure to create demand by constantly finding "customers," to create an impression of urgency to press the regional health authority into providing more funding, and to provide speedier service for those who can pay extra.

● ● ●

Demand for insured cataract surgery was so high at the Gimbel clinics that patients were waiting 12 to 13 months for treatment. The CRHA funds five ophthalmology clinics for a total of 8,000 procedures a year. It also funds 2,000 day surgeries performed in private clinics, 1,500 pregnancy terminations and about 1,500 other surgical and medical procedures. This totals about $7 million paid to 17 medical professionals and medical corporations (CRHA Backgrounder).

One of those corporations is Enterprise Universal Inc. (EUI) owned by the Huang brothers: ophthalmologist Dr. Peter Huang and otolaryngologist Dr. Ian

Huang. EUI purchased the 180-bed Holy Cross Hospital for $4.5 million in 1998 after it had been shut down by the CRHA. At the time, Peter Huang was head of ophthalmology for the CRHA and had been awarded a contract to do all Foothills Hospital's cataract surgery in his private clinic.

The CRHA stripped the Holy Cross Hospital of all medical equipment, including the $40 million operating rooms installed shortly before the closure. Nevertheless, $4.5 million seemed low for the inner city property and buildings. The City of Calgary estimated that a 90-car parking lot across the street which was requisitioned by the hospital in 1993 was worth at least $3 million (Walker, 1998).

According to CRHA officials, the Huangs' original bid was rejected because its wording suggested the development may continue to receive money from the CRHA when the health body wanted no financial ties to any new facility. However, a few months later the CRHA awarded the Holy Cross facility a contract to perform eye, nose and throat, and foot operations. The CRHA had sold the hospital and then contracted back to the buyer for an undisclosed sum.

The lines between the publicly funded CRHA and private clinics blurred again in 1999 when the CRHA hired Dr. Kabir Jivraj to be chief medical officer for the region. Dr. Jivraj is also one of the owners of Surgical Centres Inc., which six weeks earlier had been awarded a CRHA acute-care services contract to do 2,000 procedures. CRHA spokesman Roman Cooney confirmed that the contract to perform ear, nose, throat and orthopedic procedures was one of three contracts the firm holds with the CRHA, but he denied that Dr. Jivraj, one of four partners in Surgical Centres Inc., had been part of the discussions concerning the contract. Mr. Cooney also refused to reveal the value of the contracts, citing Freedom of Information and Privacy rules that exempt disclosure of commercial contracts entered into by public bodies (Marshall). For his part, Dr. Jivraj said he intended to resign from the board of Surgical Centres Inc. when he assumed his new $250,000 a year position with the CRHA.

The CRHA's next major contracting venture with private providers appears likely to be for MRI scans. MRIs provide doctors with a tool that accurately and easily maps soft body tissues, thereby improving diagnoses for such things as brain, spinal cord, and joint injuries. The machine places the patient in a strong magnetic field; radio waves are then focused on the body part being examined. The reaction of the patient's cells to the two fields is measured, and computers use the data to construct a detailed, three-dimensional model of the area. There are other methods that do the same thing, but MRI does it without needles, without radiation, and without injections.

Both doctors and patients like the definitive diagnosis that an MRI provides. But the cost of the machines—$2.5 million each—has meant that for several years now demand has outstripped supply in the publicly funded system. People with potentially serious illnesses have to wait and worry for months.

Calgary's private MRI clinic, Western Canada MRI Centre, is owned by a group of doctors and investors: Elliott, Fong, Wallace and Associates. Dr. Chen Fong was head of radiology at Foothills at the same time he was medical director for Western Canada MRI (*Western Report*, 7 June 1993). He is now head of radiology for the CRHA.

In 1996, after the CRHA had decided to close the Bow Valley Centre, CRHA officials seriously considered selling a brand-new MRI scanner that had recently been installed in the hospital to Western Canada MRI and then contracting to the company for services. When several radiologists at the doomed hospital objected, the MRI was moved to the Peter Lougheed Hospital. But while the MRI was out of commission during the move, the CRHA referred urgent MRI cases to the Western Canada private clinic at the CRHA's expense.

In December 1999, shortly after Premier Klein announced his intention to introduce legislation allowing for-profit private hospitals, the CRHA issued a request for proposals from private-sector partners interested in providing and operating MRIs at the Alberta Children's Hospital, Rockyview Hospital, and Foothills Hospital. According to the CRHA press release, "The current waiting list is about 200 days.... [T]imely action is required in order to have facilities capable of delivering fully operational services by Sept. 20, 2000."

All procedures and services will be covered by the CRHA through public funds and there will be no preferential access. "This is *not* privatized health care" the press release continued, emphasizing the "not." "Private MRIs are already provided by the private sector. We are proposing a contract with the private sector to offer the same service on behalf of the CRHA for hospital in-patients at our sites." Now the MRIs in hospitals would be owned and operated by the private sector.

The press release was signed by Dr. Kabir Jivraj, the CRHA's recently appointed executive vice-president and Chief Medical Officer.

11
QUESTIONS AND
ANSWERS

THE DEBATE OVER whether to increase private for-profit health care in Canada comes down to several questions, all of which are clearly answered by sound evidence.

1. ARE PRIVATE HOSPITALS CHEAPER AND MORE EFFICIENT THAN PUBLIC ONES?

No. In fact, they are *more expensive* and *less efficient*. The evidence on this speaks loudly and with one voice. When a major scientific journal such as the *New England Journal of Medicine* says bluntly that in decades of research, "No peer-reviewed study has found that for-profit hospitals are less expensive," it is not leaving much to the imagination (Woolhandler and Himmelstein, 1999). Since at least the 1960s, study after study has found that market forces in health care cause serious problems. For-profit hospitals cost more to operate, charge higher prices, spend far more on administration, and often provide poorer services than non-profit and public hospitals. And there is evidence that the cost gap between for-profit and not-for-profit, public health care appears to be widening. The reasons for these problems are plain; here are a few of them:

- Investors in for-profit health care normally expect profits in the range of 15 percent annually.

- Executive teams and managers in for-profit facilities, in addition to operating a health-care facility, must devote substantial time, staff, and money to investor relations, take-over strategies and defences, marketing, corporate filings, securities requirements, insurance administration, and bill collections.

- Stock options and other incentives for staff in for-profit facilities add expense, and they fuel a powerful vested interest among executives and clinicians that helps drive up demand for services, revenues, and—in the process—costs.

- There is costly duplication of equipment and facilities in for-profit hospitals and clinics, because each must compete with every other hospital and clinic. As a result, equipment and facilities are less efficiently used in for-profit health care.

- For-profit facilities must pay for marketing.

- For-profit facilities must pay income taxes.

2. DO MARKET FORCES WORK WITH HEALTH CARE LIKE THEY DO WITH PRODUCTS SUCH AS FOOD AND CONSUMER GOODS?

No. Virtually every health economist concedes that market forces do not work in health care as they do in other areas. In fact, health care is widely regarded by economists as a case of market failure. The signs of this failure are widespread. In the US, where market-driven medicine is most powerful, the costs of health care are highest. In Calgary, where the costs of cataract surgery are the highest in Alberta, the waiting lists are the longest; in Britain, the introduction of market forces led to the biggest jump in public spending on health care in decades.

Health care does not lend itself to competition, for several reasons. Patients are often unable to comparison shop, and it is not easy to substitute one product for another. Patients are frequently unable to make well-informed decisions on their own, and typically the bigger and more costly the decision the less well-informed patients are able to be. People cannot return medical procedures for a refund, or make exchanges, or take "test drives." The role of the consumer is hampered because (for understandable reasons) people do not have direct access to prescription drugs and specialists, and cannot admit themselves to hospitals.

The advantages doctors enjoy over patients in knowledge, health, and access to resources, mean that patients are unduly vulnerable to manipulation. Extensive evidence shows that doctors, when motivated by financial rewards, can create unnecessary demand for their services. For-profit health care feeds this problem, escalating health care costs more rapidly than under public systems.

3. WILL FOR-PROFIT HEALTH CARE RAISE COSTS TO THE PUBLIC SYSTEM?

Yes. The inefficiencies, conflicts of interest, and other problems inevitable in for-profit medicine drive up the costs of the public system. In the US, tax-financed public spending on hospitals, physicians, home health care, and other health services is 13 to 16 percent costlier in regions where for-profit hospitals are common than in regions without for-profit hospitals (Silverman,

Skinner, and Fisher).

For-profit health care cannot flourish without public subsidies. In Canada, for-profit health care companies relentlessly pursue taxpayer money. In the US, which has the largest for-profit health sector in the world, Americans now pay more *in taxes* for health care than do Canadians. In addition, Americans face large private insurance premiums, user fees, and out-of-pocket costs; and they still have a system in which about 40 million people go uninsured.

The evidence is overwhelming that for-profit health-care providers do not compete by lowering costs or improving efficiencies. Instead, they impress customers with often-excessive use of technologies. They create a "star system" among doctors that drives up all physicians' salaries. They specialize in the least-complicated and lowest-risk procedures, leaving the more-difficult and more-expensive cases in the public system.

4. WHAT EFFECT DO PRIVATE CLINICS HAVE ON WAITING LISTS?

They often make them *longer*. Long waiting lists are a serious problem for people in pain or in deteriorating health, but waiting lists occur for many reasons. There may not be enough money to meet the need, or there may be a shortage of nurses, doctors, or technologists (an increasingly common problem across Canada and internationally). And, unfortunately, waiting lists as a measure of service capacity are notoriously unreliable. People may be placed on waiting lists "just in case" they need the procedure; institutions or doctors sometimes pad waiting lists to build cases for more money or facilities (Rachlis and Kushner); and sometimes people don't want a procedure immediately, preferring to be booked for a more convenient time in the future.

Dollar for dollar, the most-efficient health-care system will have the shortest waiting lists. Channelling public money to the less-efficient private system is a wasteful way to address waiting lists. Eye surgery, much of which is done in private clinics, provides a good example:

- Waiting lists are longest and costs are highest for cataract surgery in Alberta in centres where the proportion of private clinics is highest:

    a) In Calgary, where the most surgeons work, and where all cataract surgery is done in private facilities, Albertans had a 56 percent chance of having cataract surgery in less than 12 weeks.

    b) In Edmonton, where most cataract surgery is done in public facilities, Albertans had an 87 percent chance of having surgery in less than 12 weeks.

    c) In Lethbridge, where all cataract surgery is done in public facilities, 100 percent of patients had surgery in less than 12 weeks (Consumers Association of Canada—Alberta Branch, March 1999).

- In Manitoba, waiting lists for cataract surgery were twice as long with surgeons who operated in both the private and public systems, in comparison to surgeons who did all their operations in the public system. The study found waiting lists of surgeons who operated only in public facilities were seven to ten weeks. In contrast, surgeons who operated in both public and private facilities had waiting lists of

14 to 23 weeks for operations in public facilities. Surgeons typically billed $1,000 extra per patient if the surgery was done in a private facility (Manitoba Centre for Health Policy and Evaluation).

If the waiting list for a medical procedure is too long, then committing more resources to that procedure ought to shorten the waiting list. Since the public system makes more efficient use of resources than the private one, committing those additional resources to the public system will shorten waiting lists more quickly than committing more resources to the private system. For example, figures from the Alberta Workers' Compensation Board show it will pay $3,602 to do two knee surgeries in private clinics; for the same cost *nine* of the same knee surgeries can be done in a public facility, and the public facility would still break even ("Claimant Services Herald," October 1998, Alberta Workers Compensation Board; *Edmonton Journal*, 29 Nov. 1999, pB1).

Increasing funds to the private system can actually lengthen waiting lists if those funds would otherwise have gone to the public system, because an efficient service provider is being replaced by an inefficient one. Using the example of knee surgery, transferring $3,600 into the private system from the public one could add seven people to the waiting list for knee surgery: two will get their operation instead of nine, leaving seven to wait.

The larger the private health-care industry, the louder the claim of its lobbying voice for public health-care funds. The more those funds go to the private system the less efficient health care will be, and the longer its waiting lists.

5. Were health care costs skyrocketing before the Klein government cuts?

Absolutely not. Premier Klein, his cabinet ministers, and various government officials repeatedly claimed that health-care costs were rising uncontrollably in the years before his government launched its cuts. This is not true. By any reliable measure there was no significant increase in per-capita spending on health care in Alberta under the government of Don Getty.

6. Is the aging of the baby boomers going to doom medicare?

Health costs gradually rise as people age, particularly when people reach their seventies and beyond. The first baby boomers will reach their seventies in the year 2016, and the peak of the baby boom will hit their early seventies in about 2030. The impact of the aging baby boomers on the health-care system is predictable and there is plenty of time to prepare. As some health economists say, the baby boom is a glacier, not an avalanche. It will add more costs to health care, but it need not create a threat to medicare. Careful analyses of health spending show that it is not so much the aging of our population that affects health-care spending, as the fact that our health-care responses to aging are often poorly managed. For example, we have historically emphasized institutional care over home care for the elderly, though home care is less expensive and frequently more appropriate (Barer, Evans, and Hertzman).

The aging of baby boomers should lead us, as individuals and as a society, to embrace medicare all the more. Medicare is more efficient and equitable than private care, so the most cost-effective way to respond to the rising health costs of an aging population is to strengthen medicare, including establishing a national home care program based on the principles of the Canada Health Act. The real threat to medicare is misguided government policy that erodes public health care and increases the role of for-profit medicine.

7. IS MEDICARE AN ECONOMIC ADVANTAGE FOR CANADA?

Yes. On 15 April 1999, Charles Baillie, Chairman and CEO of the Toronto-Dominion Bank, gave a major speech to the Vancouver Board of Trade. "Canada's health care system is an economic asset, not a burden," he told the audience, "one that today, more than ever, our country dare not lose...." Over and over he pointed out the strengths of Canada's medicare system. Though he fully recognized that medicare must adapt to new conditions, he came down strongly in its defence. While many of his remarks addressed the moral value of medicare, some of his most pointed comments concerned the importance of its economic efficiency:

> *It would cost every business, large and small, more if they had to pay for benefits themselves. It would, in a very real sense, constitute a de facto increase in taxation—for employers or for employees or both... [I]n an era of globalization, we need every competitive and comparative advantage we have. And the fundamentals of our health care system are one of those advantages.* (Baillie).

As Baillie understands, the comparative efficiency of Canada's medicare system is good for the whole economy. If for-profit health care grows in Canada, it will lead to higher overall costs, weakening one of Canada's trade advantages. In 1988, Chrysler estimated that it spent US$700 on health benefits for every car it produced in the US, but only US$233 for each car it made in Canada (Rachlis and Kushner). The magazine *Scientific American* reported in 1993 that health-insurance premiums added more than $2,000 to the price of an average automobile manufactured in the United States (Wallich and Holloway). Health care benefits are usually incidental in labour negotiations in Canada (though this may change with more privatization), but they are frequently the biggest pitfall in US labour negotiations, being the key factor in 55 percent of strikes and lockouts there in 1990 (Rachlis and Kushner).

8. DO KLEIN'S PROPOSALS THREATEN CANADA'S MEDICARE BECAUSE OF THE NORTH AMERICAN FREE TRADE AGREEMENT?

Yes, there are threats. Of all the long-term implications of the Klein government's proposals, none raises more worrisome concerns than those relating to NAFTA, the North American Free Trade Agreement. NAFTA is an agreement signed in 1993 by Canada, the United States, and Mexico to establish and enforce rules concerning trade and investment among the three countries.

Barry Appleton, the managing partner of Appleton and Associates International Lawyers, based in Toronto and New York City, captures the basic conflict between medicare and NAFTA in one sentence: "At its very heart the NAFTA protects the logic of the free market: an idea which inevitably conflicts with the nature of Canada's health care system" (Appleton, p87). The spirit of NAFTA and the spirit of Canada's health-care system do not mix.

The Canadian government recognized this problem when it negotiated the terms of the agreement, and there is some protection for health care in the terms of NAFTA. Unfortunately the wording of this protection is unclear, and is open to competing interpretations. This is made more confusing because NAFTA is not governed by Canadian law but by international law, which defines terms differently than we do within Canada.

The concern expressed by Appleton and other experts (see, for example, Schwartz, Bryan) is that once the door is opened to private hospitals it may become very difficult to close. Premier Klein's proposals may not be merely an experiment; they may be irreversible. Appleton, in an extensive and important article on NAFTA and health care, says this:

> *The NAFTA is structured to protect and encourage government measures that increase access to markets. This results in the NAFTA irreversibly protecting the trend towards private health care while eroding the ability of governments to reverse this trend.*

Suppose the Calgary Regional Health Authority contracts with surgical companies to provide major orthopedic surgeries such as hip replacements. Then suppose costs begin to rise, waiting lists lengthen, and efficiency suffers, so that the CRHA is paying more money for less services than other parts of the province. What happens if the CRHA wants to return to providing some of these same services itself? NAFTA might come into play. If, for example, one of the surgical companies were backed by a venture capital fund that had even one American or Mexican investor, that investor could file a claim under NAFTA against the Canadian government. (Canadians could not file a claim; amazingly, under NAFTA, foreigners have more rights than nationals). The claim would be that the Alberta government, through the CRHA, was cutting into and harming the business of the surgical corporation, taking away its customers and market share, and reducing its profits. Appleton explains:

> *If governmental action harmed an investor's property (such as market share or goodwill), that investor could make a claim for expropriation under the NAFTA.*
>
> *Thus, whenever government leaves an area of health care to the private sector, its return will invariably be costly.* (p93)

The expropriation rules under NAFTA are more generous to investors than they are under Canadian law. So in the example above, the Canadian or Alberta governments, or the CRHA, might be required under NAFTA to compensate the surgical corporation for the value of its assets, *and for lost potential profits*. This means that Alberta taxpayers could be on the hook not just for actual profits, but profits the company *might* have made if it hadn't lost market share when the CRHA returned to providing surgery directly. It's little wonder Appleton says, "[T]he broad compensation commitments of the NAFTA ensure that government privatization will be a one-way process" (p100).

The most serious challenges to Canadian medicare are likely to come from American corporations. The respected British medical journal *The Lancet* quotes with concern a major US industry group—The Coalition of Service Industries—that wants to expand business in health services to foreign markets:

> *Historically, health care services in many foreign countries have largely been the responsibility of the public sector.*

> *This public ownership of health care has made it difficult for US private-sector health care providers to market in foreign countries....* (Price, Pollock, and Shaoul)

A senior US trade official quoted in *The Lancet* explains the American agenda for health care outside the US:

> *The United States is of the view that commercial opportunities exist along the entire spectrum of health and social care facilities, including hospitals, outpatient facilities, clinics, nursing homes, assisted living arrangements, and services provided in the home.* (Price, Pollock, and Shaoul).

NAFTA claims would be argued in long and costly legal battles, and there are no guarantees who would win. There is some protection for medicare in NAFTA, but it is ambiguous and by no means certain. The potential benefits to the public from the Klein proposals are so unlikely, and the risks are so great, that it is reckless for Alberta to proceed.

• • •

Some people wonder why health care should be in a category of its own. If everything else is sold through markets, why shouldn't health care be too? But of course, not everything else is sold through markets. Health care is a public service, as are schools, roads, police, fire protection, the military, the courts, and a wide range of other services. Sometimes these are provided as public services for reasons of efficiency, sometimes out of a commitment to fairness and justice, sometimes because we all benefit jointly from the service. If we wanted, we could privatize our streets and have companies arrange toll booths throughout our cities. We could limit police services to people who could afford the cost of investigations. Universities could arrange a marketplace for university degrees, selling them to the highest bidder. Judges could sell their decisions. We could send fire-trucks and ambulances only to those who could pay.

There are sound reasons why we don't provide everything through the marketplace. The market has its strengths, and it has its limits. If we want, health care can be opened to market forces, but costs and inefficiencies will rise, and fairness will decline. A few people will reap the benefits; the great majority will suffer the consequences. Albertans have a choice to make, and the case for the wiser choice is crystal clear. Attempting to strengthen our health-care system by turning to private, for-profit service providers is a profound mistake.

12

THE CURE IS

THE DISEASE

ON 18 DECEMBER 1999, after Premier Klein had used province-wide television to tell Albertans about his plan to allow for-profit, overnight surgical centres, after he had published personal editorials in both *Time* magazine and the *Globe and Mail* arguing for a larger role for for-profit health care, and after he had made speeches and sparred in legislative debates on the topic, the Premier's Minister of Health and Wellness, Halvar Jonson, wrote in a letter-to-the-editor in the *Edmonton Journal*, "First, government is not promoting private health care.... There is no campaign to promote any particular position; only an effort to inform and encourage input." This claim is absurd. Of course there is a campaign to promote private health care. It insults Albertans to say otherwise. Citizens cannot trust governments that deny the obvious.

From the beginning of his time as premier, Ralph Klein has broken trust with Albertans about health care. He told us spending was soaring when in fact it had been under tight control for years before he became premier. His government's cuts led to the layoffs of thousands of health-care staff, the closing of thousands of hospital beds, and the demolition of a huge Calgary hospital, and yet on a province-wide radio broadcast on 27 December 1999, he said:

The health system today is no different than it was in 1990...the situation was no different then than today. The only difference is that we...took 200 hospital jurisdictions and reorganized those into 17. We cut administration costs, and that's where most of the cuts took place. (CBC Radio)

Despite Mr. Klein's claims, the health system today is markedly different than it was in 1990, and ironically many of those differences are now used as reasons to open the system to private, for-profit, acute-care service providers.

Trust is at the heart of the debate over public versus private health care. People in need of health care must be able to trust that their weakness will not be exploited. Will we be able to trust for-profit clinics and hospitals to serve our needs above their own? Will we be able to trust our doctor's advice? Will we be able to trust our government when it says it wants to protect our public health-care system?

● ● ●

The Klein government has said it can reduce the aches and pains of Alberta's health-care system—and of Albertans—by turning over more services to for-profit businesses. There is no doubt that Alberta's health-care system needs help, but volumes of evidence make it clear that turning to for-profit medicine will make things worse. This has already been seen in Alberta with cataract surgery: the larger the portion of cataract surgery done in private clinics the higher the patient charges and the longer the waiting lists. The government now wants to take the same approach to hip and knee surgery.

The cure offered to Canada's medicare system by for-profit medicine is no cure at all, but it remains the Klein government's treatment of choice. Since shortly after Ralph Klein became premier, there has been a step-by-step increase in the privatization of health care in Alberta. When asked on national television in December 1999 if his government's proposed legislation is "your next step towards, as many people might suspect, privatization [of medicare]," Mr. Klein replied:

The one step was taken many years ago. The one step was taken with cataract surgeries; the one step was taken when the Canada Health Act opened it up to private abortion clinics; the one step was taken when hospital authorities, health authorities were able to contract with diagnostic services. Those steps were taken a long time ago. (CBC TV, Dec. 6, 1999)

There is no reason to believe that the government's current proposals for private surgery will be the last step in the privatization of health care. And with each step the system becomes more troubled, sicker. In Calgary, where privatization has been taken furthest, the troubles have been the greatest, the deficits largest, the waiting lists longest, the potential conflicts of interest most worrisome, the patient charges highest. More and more, it is clear that the Klein government's cure is, in fact, the disease.

APPENDIX A: THE NUMBERS BEHIND THE GRAPHS

MUCH OF THE KLEIN government's campaign to cut public spending, including the Premier's 1997 province-wide television address, has been based on some very convincing but utterly misleading statistics that can be traced to a set of briefing notes prepared by internal staff for cabinet in the spring of 1992, in the last days of the Getty government.

In those briefing notes is a graph that has three lines on it, running from 1981 to 1993. (A copy of the original is shown here as Graph 'A'.) On the graph, all numbers have been converted to percentages so they can be compared. One line shows Alberta's population growth creeping slowly upward; a second line shows inflation gradually rising; and a third line shows spending on health care zooming, leaving inflation and population growth far behind. This graph sends a compelling message of out-of-control spending: while inflation and population growth are low, spending on health care is soaring. Once Ralph Klein became Premier, the message from this graph became a crucial piece of propaganda. Before long, variations of it were circulating widely, influencing politicians, bureaucrats, business people, the media, and leaders in the medical

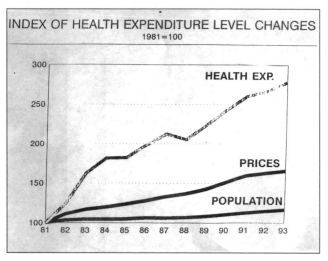

INDEX OF HEALTH EXPENDITURE LEVEL CHANGES
1981=100

GRAPH A

community. Though it only covered health spending, the government used it to imply that all services were in the same situation. This graph was a kind of lucky charm for the Conservative agenda; showing it to the public seemed to justify every cut.

The problem is that Graph A is a statistical sham. Intuitively it makes good sense, but then, intuitively the Earth is flat. This graph creates a kind of optical illusion. It is not that the numbers are wrong, it is that they have been incompletely calculated.

The very same briefing notes that contained Graph A also contained a graph that showed the correct interpretation of the numbers. A copy of this is shown here as Graph B. This graph contains two lines. It may be hard to believe, but *the line labelled 'Health' in Graph B is based on the same numbers that are in Graph A.*

The different impressions created by the two graphs can be explained by calculating the relationships among inflation, population growth, and spending on health care. To do this, inflation must be multiplied by population growth. When this is done, it turns out that after 1983, the level of inflation per person is almost exactly the same as the rise in health expenditures per person. In other words, after 1983, health expenditures per person in Alberta barely changed in real dollars.

As Graph B correctly presents, the entire real increase in health-care spending occurred in the early 1980s, almost 20 years ago. Despite the claims of Ralph Klein, there was no real change in per capita spending on health care for almost ten years *before* any of his cuts began in 1993.

It is worth noting the second line on Graph B, which is labelled 'other programs'. It illustrates the downward trends in spending on all public services other than health care, *before* the Klein cuts. This includes, among

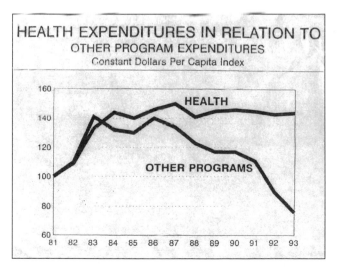

GRAPH B

other things, education, social services, and transportation. The Klein government has rarely discussed specifics about historical spending in these areas.

On its own this information does not mean Alberta was spending too little, enough, or too much on public services. In a democracy that is for voters to decide. In 1983, Alberta was spending more than other provinces on public services; by 1992 most other provinces had caught up or passed it. The crucial point here is that Albertans were not given accurate information, and therefore could not draw an informed conclusion. They were told that spending was soaring when it was not. The democratic processes upon which an electorate depends to cast an informed vote, and which are the shared responsibility of the government, opposition, media, and public interest groups, badly broke down. Would Albertans have supported the Klein government's cutbacks from 1993 to 1995 if they had been truthfully told that spending on health care had not changed in real terms for a decade, and that spending on other public services had already been declining for years? We will never know; Albertans were never given the chance.

Graph A (and its many variations put out by the government) is so convincing that it is reasonable to assume the Klein cabinet believes it is the truth, though any credible economist will confirm it is not. And that leads to the disconcerting thought that the cuts to health care, education, roads, social services, culture, and the environment, may have all been a kind of accident. It may be that in a cabinet containing some powerful anti-government ideologues, no one stopped for a moment of sober second thought. This possibility was made clear to me when I discussed the differences between Graphs A and B with a class at the University of Alberta. Afterwards a member of the audience who had held a senior position in the Government of Alberta during the cutbacks came up to me in disbelief and asked me to repeat my explanation of the graphs. Clearly, until that moment, he hadn't understood how mistaken Graph A was. He mulled the material over, shook his head gently to himself, and quietly left.

Kevin Taft

APPENDIX B:

TRENDS IN

PROVINCIAL

GOVERNMENT

HEALTH SPENDING

THE TABLE ON the next page shows spending levels by provincial governments on health care. In 1996, Alberta's spending per person on health care was about 12% higher than in 1976, adjusting for inflation. Alberta had the highest levels of spending among all provinces in 1976, 1981, and 1986, and was second highest in 1991. In 1996, Alberta's spending was below the Canadian average, and third lowest among all provinces, just below the levels of Newfoundland., Prince Edward Island, Manitoba, and Saskatchewan. Alberta actually reached its highest level of spending on health care in 1990, at $1,411 per person; the cuts of the Klein government reached deepest in 1995, when spending was $1,156 per person (constant 1986 dollars). Since 1996, spending on health care has increased in Alberta, but final calculations on the extent of the increase depend on population and inflation-rate data and were not available at the time of writing.

PROVINCIAL GOVERNMENT SPENDING
ON HEALTH CARE
per capita, constant 1986 dollars

	1976	1981	1986	1991	1996
Alberta	$1,066	$1,114	$1,360	$1,366	$1,201
B.C.	$875	$1,053	$1,141	$1,278	$1,233
Sask.	$922	$964	$1,184	$1,312	$1,219
Man.	$999	$1,013	$1,160	$1,276	$1,217
Ont.	$1,003	$1,033	$1,160	$1,406	$1,416
Quebec	$998	$1,013	$1,143	$1,234	$1,164
N.B.	$827	$959	$1,043	$1,286	$1,267
N.S.	$849	$913	$1,028	$1,180	$1,045
P.E.I.	$928	$940	$1,022	$1,154	$1,212
Nfld.	$852	$931	$1,057	$1,163	$1,212
Cdn. Av.	$975	$1,025	$1,163	$1,322	$1,279

SOURCE:

CANADIAN INSTITUTE FOR HEALTH INFORMATION, 1998

APPENDIX C:

HEALTH SPENDING

AS A PORTION

OF GDP

A COMMON WAY to assess health-care spending is to measure it as a percentage of a country's or province's gross domestic product (GDP). This reveals the percentage of overall economic activity in a country or province that is devoted to health care.

By this measure, total spending on health care for Canada as a whole peaked in 1992, at 10 percent of GDP. It fell during most of the 1990s, and by 1998 was estimated at 9.1 percent of GDP. The equivalent figure for the US is about 14 percent of GDP.

In Alberta, total spending on health care as a percent of GDP fell steadily and rather sharply through the 1990s, from 8.8 percent in 1992, to an estimated 7.0 percent in 1998. (Earlier and later figures are not yet available.) This decline reflects not only the cuts to health spending by the Alberta government, but the growth in the overall level of economic activity in the province. (Canadian Institute of Health Information, 1998)

BIBLIOGRAPHY

Agretelis, Joan (1997) "For Our Patients, Not for Profits". *Journal of the American Medical Association*, 3 December 1997, Vol.278, No.21, pp 1733–1734.

Alberta Department of Health and Wellness, Government of Alberta website, January 2000.

Alberta Department of Health (1998) "Health Workforce Adjustment Strategy Project Report", Government of Alberta, February 1998, p11.

Alberta Hansard, 1 December 1999, Government of Alberta.

Alberta Hansard, 25 October 1995, Government of Alberta.

Alberta Hansard, 18 October 1994, Government of Alberta.

Altman, Stuart H., and David Shactman (1997) "Should We Worry About Hospitals' High Administrative Costs?". *New England Journal of Medicine*, 13 March 1997, 336:798–799.

Anderson, Gerard F. (1997) "The Role of Investment bankers in Nonprofit Conversions." *Health Affairs*, March/April 1997, Vol 16, No.2, pp 144–147.

Appleton, Barry (1999) "International Agreements and National Health Plans: NAFTA", p87–104, in Drache, Daniel, and Terry Sullivan, eds., *Health Reform*. London: Routledge.

Auditor General of Alberta (1999) *Annual Report of The Auditor General of Alberta, 1998–99*. Edmonton: Government of Alberta.

Badgley, Robin F., and R. David Smith (1979) *User Charges for Health Services*. Toronto: The Ontario Council of Health.

Badgley, Robin F., and Samuel Wolfe (1967) *Doctor's Strike*. Toronto: The Macmillan Company.

Baillie, Charles A. (1999) "Health Care in Canada: Preserving a Competitive Advantage". Speech to The Vancouver Board of Trade, 15 April 1999. The Toronto-Dominion Bank.

Barer, Morris L., Robert G. Evans, and Clyde Hertzman (1995) "Avalanche or Glacier?: Health Care and the Demographic Rhetoric", *Canadian Journal on Aging*, Vol. 14, No. 2, pp 193–224.

Barer, M.L., R.G. Evans, and G.L. Stoddart (1979) *Controlling Health Care Costs by Direct Charges to Patients: Snare or Delusion?* Toronto: Ontario Economic Council.

Blomquist, Ake (1995) "Reforming Health Care: Canada and the Second Wave", p165–191, in Jerome-Forget, Monique, Joseph White, and Joshua M. Wiener, eds., *Health Care Reform Through Internal Markets*. The Institute for Research on Public Policy/ The Brookings Institution.

Blomquist, Ake (1979) *The International Health Care Business*. Vancouver: The Fraser Institute.

Braid, Don (1994) *Calgary Herald*, 9 August 1994.

Canadian Institute for Health Information (1998) *National Health Expenditure Trends, 1975–1998*. Ottawa: Canadian Institute for Health Information.

Canadian Medical Discoveries Fund Inc. (1999) *1999 Annual Report*.

Clarkson, Kenneth (1972) "Some Implications of Property Rights in Hospital Management". *Journal of Law and Economics*, 15:363–384.

Claxton, Gary, et al. (1997) "Public Policy Issues in Nonprofit Conversions: An Overview". *Health Affairs*, March/April 1997, Vol 16, No.2, pp 9–28.

Consumers' Association of Canada (Alberta Branch) (May 1999) "Patient Charges for 'Enhanced' Cataract Lens", and "Waiting Times for Publicly Insured Cataract Surgery", information bulletin.

Consumers' Association of Canada (Alberta Branch) (March, 1999) "Provincial Consumer Survey on Access to Cataract Surgery casts Doubt on Claims by Private Health Interests", press release and "Backgrounder".

CRHA Backgrounder (1999) "Partnerships with Non-Profit and Private Health Service Providers", 5 December 1999, Calgary: Calgary Regional Health Authority.

CRHA (1998) *1998/1999 Annual Report*. Calgary: Calgary Regional Health Authority.

Crowley, Brian Lee, David Zitner, Nancy Faraday-Smith (1999) *Operating in the Dark: The Gathering Crisis in Canada's Public Health Care System*. Atlantic Institute for Market Studies. Halifax, Nova Scotia.

Edmonton Journal, 29 November 1999, "Private Surgery Slammed: Contracting out costs WCB more than medicare", pB1.

Edmonton Journal, 20 November 1999, "Results of Pilot Project for Private Clinics still Unclear", pA7.

Evans, Robert G. (1997) "Going for the Gold: The Redistributive Agenda behind Market-Based Health Care Reform", *Journal of Health Politics, Policy and Law*, April 1997, Vol. 22, No. 2, pp 427–465.

Fellows, C. Michael, Greg Flanagan, and Stanford Shedd (1997) *Economic Issues: A Canadian Perspective*. Toronto: McGraw-Hill Ryerson.

Ferrier, Gary D., and Vivian Valdmanis (1996) "Rural Hospital Performance and its Correlates". *Journal of Productivity Analysis*, 7:63–80.

Fuller, Colleen (1999a) "Partnering for profit, undermining Medicare: A comprehensive investigation of MDS Inc." Vancouver: Hospital Employees' Union.

Fuller, Colleen (1999b) "HRG Health Resources Group Inc. and NAFTA", November, 1999, unpublished paper.

Fuller, Colleen (1998) *Caring For Profit*. Vancouver: New Star Books.

Garg, Pushkal P., Kevin D. Frick, Marie Diener-West, Neil R. Powe (1999) "Effect of the Ownership of Dialysis Facilities on Patients' Survival and Referral for Transplantation". *New England Journal of Medicine* (25 November 1999) Vol. 341, No. 22.

Geddes, Ashley (1999) *Edmonton Journal*, 13 December 1999.

Gimbel, Karen (1999) "As Canadian As Medicare". Speech by Karen Gimbel to Strategic Leadership Forum, Calgary, 12 May 1999.

Glennester, Howard (1995) "Internal Markets: Context and Structure", pp17–26, in Jerome-Forget, Monique, Joseph White, and Joshua M. Wiener, eds., *Health Care Reform Through Internal Markets*. The Institute for Research on Public Policy/ The Brookings Institution.

Gold, William (1994) *Calgary Herald*, 21 July 1994.

Gratzer, David (1999) *Code Blue*. Toronto: ECW Press.

Gray, Bradford H. (1997) "Conversions of HMOs and Hospitals: What's at Stake?", *Health Affairs*, March/April 1997, Vol 16, No.2, pp 29–47.

Gray, Bradford H., and Walter J. McNerney (1986a) "Special Report: For-Profit Enterprise in Health Care". *New England Journal of Medicine* (1986) 314: pp 1523–8.

Gray, Bradford H., ed. (1986b) *For-Profit Enterprise in Health Care*. Washington, D.C.: National Academy Press.

Gray, Charlotte (1996) *Saturday Night*, March 1996.

Hasan, Malik M. (1996) "Sounding Board—Let's End the Nonprofit Charade". *New England Journal of Medicine* (18 April 1996) 334:16 pp 1055–7.

Health Savvy, May 1996.

Herbert, Michael (1997) "A For-Profit Health Plan's Experience and Strategy." *Health Affairs*, March/April 1997, Vol 16, No.2, pp 121–124.

Himmelstein, David U., et al. (1999) "Quality of Care in Investor-Owned vs. Not-for-Profit HMOs". *Journal of the American Medical Association*, 14 July 1999, Vol. 282, No.2, pp 159–163.

Hoerger, Thomas J. (1991) "'Profit' Variability in For-Profit and Not-for-Profit Hospitals". Journal of Health Economics, 10:259–289.

Hollis, Steven R. (1997) "Strategic and Economic Factors in the Hospital Conversion Process." *Health Affairs*, March/April 1997, Vol. 16, No.2, pp 131–143.

HRG Health Resources Group (1999a) "Income Statement Analysis," March 1999.

HRG Health Resources Group (1999b) "Minutes, HRG Board Meeting, March 25, 1999."

HRG Health Resources Group (1999c) "Minutes, HRG Board Meeting, April 30, 1999."

HRG Health Resources Group Inc. (1997) "A Plan for the Organization and Delivery of Complementary Health Services in Canada", April 1997, Calgary.

Hsiao, William C. (1995) "Medical Savings Accounts." *Health Affairs*, Summer 1995, Vol. 14, No.2, pp 260–266.

Jerome-Forget, Monique, Joseph White, and Joshua M. Wiener, eds. (1995) *Health Care Reform Through Internal Markets*. The Institute for Research on Public Policy/ The Brookings Institution.

Lavis, John N, et al. (1998) "Free-standing health care facilities: financial arrangements, quality assurance and a pilot study". *Canadian Medical Association Journal* (10 February 1998) 158 (3), pp 359–363.

Levinsky, Norman G. (1999) "Quality and Equity in Dialysis and Renal Transplantation". *New England Journal of Medicine* (25 November 1999) Vol. 341, No. 22.

Light, Donald (1993a) "Conclusion: Lessons From Managed Competition in Britain", in Light, Donald, and Annabelle May (1993) *Britain's Health System: From Welfare State to Managed Markets*, pp 161–172. Washington: Faulkner and Gray.

Light, Donald, and Annabelle May (1993) *Britain's Health System: From Welfare State to Managed Markets*. Washington: Faulkner and Gray.

Lisac, Mark (1995) *Edmonton Journal*, 8 June 1995.

Manitoba Centre for Health Policy and Evaluation (1998) "Waiting
    Times for Surgery in Manitoba." Report summary by R.J. Currie,
    based on a report by Carolyn De Coster et al. July, 1998.
Marshall, Andy (1999) *Calgary Herald*, 18 October 1999.
May, Annabelle (1993) "Thatcherism, the New Public Management,
    and the NHS", in Light, Donald, and Annabelle May (1993b)
    Britain's Health System: From Welfare State to Managed Markets, pp
    21–28. Washington: Faulkner and Gray.
Maynard, Alan (1995) "Internal Markets and Health Care: A British
    Perspective", p27–47, in Jerome-Forget, Monique, Joseph
    White, and Joshua M. Wiener, eds. (1995) *Health Care Reform
    Through Internal Markets*. The Institute for Research on Public
    Policy/ The Brookings Institution.
McArthur, William (1999) "Making Hospitals Work for Patients",
    Fraser Forum, February 1999, pp 5–6. Vancouver: The Fraser
    Institute.
MDS Inc. (1998) *1998 Annual Report*.
Mertl, Steve (1999) "Pressure to spend mounting, Klein says",
    Edmonton Journal, 11 May 1999, pA7.
Miller, Linda B. (1997) "The Conversion Game: High Stakes, Few
    Rules." *Health Affairs*, March/April 1997, Vol 16, No.2, pp
    112–117.
Nagle, Patrick (1994) *Vancouver Sun*, 9 May 1994.
Nelson, Barry (1999) *Calgary Herald*, 4 July 1999.
Pattison, Robert V., and Hallie M. Katz (1983) "Investor-owned and
    Not-for-Profit Hospitals: A Comparison Based on California
    Data". *New England Journal of Medicine* (1983) 309: 347–53.
Pauly, Mark V. (1997) "Who Was That Straw Man Anyway? A
    Comment on Evans and Price". *Journal of Health Politics, Policy
    and Law*, April 1997, Vol. 22, No. 2, pp 467–473.
Pedersen, Rick (1995) *Edmonton Journal*, 23 November 1995.
Peterson, Mark A. (1997) "Health Care into the Next Century".
    Journal of Health Politics, Policy and Law, April 1997, Vol. 22, No.
    2, pp 291–314.
Pommer, Dave (1995) *Calgary Herald*, 17 November 1995.
Price, David, Allyson Pollock, and Jean Shaoul (1994) "How the
    World Trade Organization is Shaping Domestic Policies in
    Health Care." *The Lancet*, November 1999, Vol. 354, No.9193.
Rachlis, Michael, and Carol Kushner (1994) *Strong Medicine*.
    Toronto: HarperCollins.
Relman, Arnold S. (1992) "What Market Values are Doing to
    Medicine." *Atlantic Monthly*, March 1992, pp 99–106.

Renn, Steven C., Carl J. Schramm, J. Michael Watt, and Robert A. Derzon (1985) "The Effects of Ownership and System Affiliation on the Economic Performance of Hospitals". *Inquiry*, 22:219–236.

Rice, Thomas (1997) "Can Markets Give Us the Health System we Want?". *Journal of Health Politics, Policy and Law*, April 1997, Vol. 22, No. 2, pp 383–426.

Robinson, James C., and Harold S. Luft (1985) "The Impact of Hospital Market Structure on Patient Volume, Average Lengths of Stay, and the Cost of Care". *Journal of Health Economics*. 4:333–356.

Saltman, Richard B. (1995) "The Role of Competitive Incentives in Recent Reforms of Northern European Health Systems", pp 75–94, in Jerome-Forget, Monique, Joseph White, and Joshua M. Wiener, eds. (1995) *Health Care Reform Through Internal Markets*. The Institute for Research on Public Policy/ The Brookings Institution.

Schwartz, Bryan P. (1996) "NAFTA reservations in the areas of health care." Buchwald Asper Gallagher Henteleff, Barristers and Attorneys-at-Law, Winnipeg.

Schwartz, James R. (1997) "The California Model", *Health Affairs*, March/April 1997, Vol 16, No.2, pp 96–98.

Sharpe, Sydney and Paul Bagnell (1995) *Financial Post*, 26 October 1995.

Silverman, Elaine M., Jonathan Skinner, and Elliott S. Fisher (1999) "The Association Between For-Profit Hospital Ownership and Increased Medicare Spending". *New England Journal of Medicine*, (August 5, 1999) 341:6 pp 420–426.

Staff Nurses Association (1996) "Patient Care in Region 10: Registered Nurses Professional Concerns and Solutions" (6 November 1996) p5. Source cited for figures: Alberta Health.

Statistics Canada (1998) "Inter-Corporate Ownership."

Steward, Gillian (1999a) Personal observation at Calgary Chamber of Commerce, June 23, 1999.

Steward, Gillian (1999b) Personal interview with Libby McMinn, Chairperson of the Former Grace Hospital Redevelopment Committee, Hillhurst Sunnyside Community Association, 22 December 1999.

Steward, Gillian (1999c) Personal interview with Nigel Patchett, 23 December 1999.

Taft, Kevin (1997) *Shredding the Public Interest*. Edmonton: University of Alberta Press and Parkland Institute.

Thorpe, Kenneth E. (1997) "The Health System in Transition; Care, Cost, and Coverage". *Journal of Health Politics, Policy and Law*, April 1997, Vol. 22, No. 2, pp 339–361.

Todd, Douglas (1999) "Hard-wired for kindness?". *Edmonton Journal*, 8 August 1999, pA10.

Walker, Robert (1998) *Calgary Herald*, 8 January 1998.

Walker, Robert (1996) *Calgary Herald*, 1 June 1996.

Walker, Robert (1995) *Calgary Herald*, 31 March 1995.

Walker, Robert (1994) *Calgary Herald*, 15 June 1994.

Wallich, Paul and Marguerite Holloway (1993) "Health Care without Perverse Incentives". *Scientific American*. July, 1993, p109.

Watson Wyatt Worldwide (1999) "The Calgary Regional Health Authority Organizational Review", April 1999.

Watt, J. Michael, Robert A. Derzon, Steven C. Renn, Carl J. Schramm, James S. Hahn, and George D. Pillari (1986) "The Comparative Economic Performance of Investor-Owned Chain and Not-for-Profit Hospitals". *New England Journal of Medicine*, 314: 89–96.

Wiener, Joshua M. (1995) "Managed Competition as Financing Reform: A View from the United States", p119–135, in Jerome-Forget, Monique, Joseph White, and Joshua M. Wiener, eds. (1995) *Health Care Reform Through Internal Markets*. The Institute for Research on Public Policy/ The Brookings Institution.

Wilson, Donna, ed. (1995) *The Canadian Health Care System*. Edmonton: Faculty of Nursing, University of Alberta.

Wilson, George W., and Joseph M. Jadlow (1982) "Competition, Profit Incentives, and Technical Efficiency in the Provision of Nuclear Medicine Services". *Bell Journal of Economics*. 13:472–482.

Woolhandler, Steffie, and David U. Himmelstein (1999) "When Money is the Mission—The High Costs of Investor-Owned Care". *New England Journal of Medicine*. 341:6, pp 444–446.

Woolhandler, Steffie, and David U. Himmelstein (1997) "Costs of Care and Administration at For-Profit Hospitals in the United States". *New England Journal of Medicine*. 336:769–74.

Woolhandler, Steffie, David U. Himmelstein, and James P. Lewontin (1993) "Administrative Costs in US Hospitals". *New England Journal of Medicine*. 329, pp 400–403.

Zelder, Martin (1999) "Take a Queue from Canada!", *Fraser Forum*, February 1999, pp 9–10.

ABOUT

THE AUTHORS

KEVIN TAFT holds a PhD in business, and he is the author of the bestselling book *Shredding the Public Interest*. He served for ten years in the 1970s and 1980s on two committees appointed by the Alberta cabinet to monitor and review Alberta's health-care system. His work has appeared in the *Globe and Mail*, the *Edmonton Journal*, the *Calgary Herald*, and elsewhere.

GILLIAN STEWARD has been a Calgary-based writer and journalist since the early 1970s. She was a syndicated columnist for Southam News, and was Managing Editor of the *Calgary Herald* from 1987 to 1990. Her work has appeared in *Report on Business*, *Canadian Business* magazine, and many other magazines and newspapers.

ABOUT PARKLAND

INSTITUTE

PARKLAND INSTITUTE is a non-profit research network that conducts, promotes and disseminates research in the broad tradition of Canadian political economy. The Institute operates under the auspices of the Faculty of Arts, University of Alberta, with input from academic members, as well as from church, private sector, union, professional, community and general members drawn from across Alberta.